Sch

THE LANGUAGE OF LITERATURE
General Editor: N. F. Blake
Professor of English Language and Linguistics
University of Sheffield

THE LANGUAGE OF LITERATURE
General Editor: N. F. Blake
Professor of English Language and Linguistics,
University of Sheffield

Published titles

Series Standing Order (The Language of Literature)

If you would like to receive future titles in this series as they are published, you can make use of our standing order facility. To place a standing order please contact your bookseller or, in case of difficulty, write to us at the address below with your name and address and the name of the series. Please state with which title you wish to begin your standing order. (If you live outside the United Kingdom we may not have the rights for your area, in which case we will forward your order to the publisher concerned.)

Customer Services Department, Macmillan Distribution Ltd
Houndmills, Basingstoke, Hampshire RG21 6XS, England

The Language of Twentieth-Century Poetry

LESLEY JEFFRIES

MACMILLAN

First published 1993 by
THE MACMILLAN PRESS LTD
Houndmills, Basingstoke, Hampshire RG21 2XS
and London
Companies and representatives
throughout the world

ISBN 0–333–45936–9 hardcover
ISBN 0–333–45937–7 paperback

A catalogue record for this book is available
from the British Library

10   9   8   7   6   5   4   3   2
04   03   02   01   00   99   98   97

Printed in Hong Kong

Contents

To Joan and Rod Jeffries, with love

Acknowledgements

I should like to express my appreciation to all my family and my friends and colleagues who have given me moral and practical support while this book was being written. I have received particular help on some details from Loreto Todd and Lynette Hunter of the School of English, University of Leeds, from Paul Bembridge of the School of Music and Humanities, University of Huddersfield, and from the series editor, Norman Blake, of Sheffield University. I am very grateful for this help, but remain responsible for any errors of fact or interpretation I have included. I am indebted to Dave Webb who has given this project considerable amounts of time and patience and gave invaluable help in finding lost files. Finally I should thank Sam and Ella whose patience in finding that they have no clean clothes to wear – again – has been exemplary.

The author and publishers wish to thank the following for permission to use copyright material:

André Deutsch Ltd for extracts from 'Canticle for Good Friday' from *Collected Poems* by Geoffrey Hill (1962); Faber & Faber Ltd for 'Broadcast' and extracts from 'And Bad as a Mile', 'Talking in Bed' and 'Water' from *The Whitsun Weddings* by Philip Larkin (1964); with Alfred A. Knopf, Inc. for 'A Hairline Fracture' from *The Kingfisher* by Amy Clampitt (1983), copyright © 1983 by Amy Clampitt; extracts from 'XXVII' and 'VI' from *The North Ship* by Ted Hughes (1966), and 'The Lake in the Park' from *The Collected Poems of Louis MacNeice*, ed. W.H. Auden (1964); Claire Harris for an extract from 'The Conception of Winter' from *The Conception of Winter*, Williams Wallace Publishers (1989);

Pronunciation Guide

There are a small number of phonemic symbols used in this book, to indicate sounds more accurately than is possible by orthography. Those symbols which might be unfamiliar to the reader, or might have different phonemic values to normal, are represented here.

CONSONANTS

Most of the consonantal symbols have predictable pronunciations. The following do not:

/θ/ as in *think*
/ð/ as in *there*
/ʃ/ as in *ship*
/ʒ/ as in *garage*
/ʧ/ as in *church*
/ʤ/ as in *judge*
/j/ as in *your*
/ŋ/ as in *sing*

VOWELS

The written vowels have many different pronunciations in English. The following symbols, relating to an RP (Received Pronunciation) accent, are used here:

/ɪ/ as in *bit*
/iː/ as in *feet*
/e/ as in *bed*

/a/ as in *bad*
/aː/ as in *bath*
/ʌ/ as in *cup*
/ʊ/ as in *put*
/uː/ as in *food*
/ə/ as in unstressed *the*
/ai/ as in *bright*
/ei/ as in *fate*
/aʊ/ as in *foul*
/eɜ/ as in *fair*
/ɪɜ/ as in *fear*

Introduction

This book about the language of twentieth-century poetry in English may seem rather short to some readers, given its wide-ranging title. It should be emphasised immediately that it is in no sense a comprehensive survey of twentieth-century poetry. Such a work would fill several large volumes and would certainly not be accessible as an introduction to the subject. It would also be difficult to see any pattern emerging from the mass of detail in such a work. The reader is, however, given a very brief overview of the main developments in poetry since 1900 in the opening chapter of the book. Since linguistic trends were not always obviously connected to other, politically and socially motivated movements, the remaining chapters refer to chronological developments only rarely.

This book is concerned with patterns; patterns of language use in poetry. For this reason it has avoided another possible pitfall for work of this kind which is to illustrate *only* the areas where the twentieth century differs from previous centuries. Clearly, many of the techniques and effects described in this book have their origin before 1900. Many of them will be old ideas given new life. Just a few are, as far as we know, completely new in the twentieth century. Instead of attempting a patchy picture outlining only the innovations of this century, this volume presents a survey of poetic uses of language, indicating in passing the areas where the twentieth century has diverged most obviously from previous times.

The aim of being relatively comprehensive linguistically (though not poetically) partly dictated the organisation of the book. The central chapters (2–7) deal in turn with linguistic topics (the spoken language, sound, word structure, meaning, grammar and text structure) each illustrated from a variety of poems taken from the century as a whole. The decision to organise the body of the work in this way was also partly a pedagogical one. For students whose knowledge of English language studies is limited, these chapters are a relatively painless way to acquire an understanding of the different aspects of language which can be exploited in poetry. I have dwelt most on the subtler uses of language (such as the variety of effects obtained from multiple meaning) and least on the areas which are easily recognised by the non-specialist (such as the fact that regional dialects may be used instead of or alongside Standard English). While I have not avoided linguistic terminology altogether, I have tried to keep the general reader in mind by including a glossary of the technical words as they have also explained the most unfamiliar terms as they arise.

Some readers may fear that the inevitable dismantling of poems to 'see how they work' will result in pieces of language scattered all over the workshop floor, fit only for the scrap heap. But mechanics will confirm that engines work all the better for being stripped down. I believe poems do too. If this modern metaphor disturbs the Romantic reader, they may prefer an organic, natural metaphor. Instead of seeing linguistic analysis as dissection, which destroys its object, we could see it as a yoga class. One by one we are made aware of parts of the body we normally pay little attention to. By valuing and exercising them all, the parts feel revitalised and work together even better than before.

One premise of this approach that should be made clear is that the 'text' consists not simply of the words on the page, but of an interaction between the words and the reader (or hearer). Thus, although there is usually a build-up of consensus as to the 'meaning' of a poem, some features of interpretations differ according to the reader. The last chapter of the book brings together the analytical techniques of chapters 2 to 7 in analysing three complete poems. The analysis is my own, and may differ in some respects from that of other readers.

Finally I should explain the rationale behind the examples used in this book. The observant reader will notice that many of the examples are quoted from a small number of poems. This is a deliberate policy aimed at reducing the disorientation felt when confronted by excerpts from many disparate sources. There are also a large number of supplementary quotations from a wider range of poems. I have tried to give enough context (or to paraphrase the context) to make the meaning clear. The examples as a group represent the whole of the century and include some quite recent quotations. As well as this chronological spread (which is, however, not chronologically ordered) I have attempted a rather tokenistic indication of geographical spread. Although many of the examples come from the work of British and American poets, there are small gestures toward the work of poets in West Africa, the Caribbean, Ireland and Canada. My unfamiliarity with work from other English-speaking areas of the world is the only excuse for other omissions.

Another 'bias' of the work is more intentional: I have deliberately quoted extensively from women poets wherever possible, although probably not more than their 'fair' 50 per cent. If I have overdone this positive discrimination, I am unrepentant. I am repeatedly shocked to find even quite recent 'anthologies' largely dominated by the work of male poets. Although women's volumes and women's publishing houses mean that the work of women is now more accessible, the pretence that this 'ghetto' makes up for ignoring women poets as mainstream writers is one that we cannot allow to stand. A related issue is the question of the 'canon', that is, that body of literature which is assumed to represent the 'best' work and which forms the basis of most courses. I am convinced by the argument that the canon is not founded solely on the quality of the work (whatever that means), but that there have been other excellent writing and potentially excellent writers throughout the ages which have not emerged for political or social reasons. I have quoted both from poets belonging to the twentieth-century version of the canon and from poets whose work is less well-known and remains, so far, uncanonised. I have not distinguished between these groups since the distinction is unimportant in this context except in so far as some of the poets will be on standard syllabuses and some will not.

1 Twentieth-Century Poetry in English

LINGUISTIC FASHIONS

It is clear from reading any history of poetry, including the short one in this chapter, that most general trends (or 'movements') of poetry written in English are reacting in some way to what has gone before. Often this rejection of the previous generation of poetry will involve a wistful backward glance at an earlier tradition which seems attractive partly because of its distance in time. A similar phenomenon occurs in the area of fashionable clothes. What your parents wear can usually be dismissed as ugly and old-fashioned, but at a distance of one or two generations, grand-parents and great-grandparents are often admired for their fashion sense.

Trying to characterise the language of something as diverse as poetry written in English through nearly 100 years is a huge, and almost impossible, task. The twentieth century is more difficult to analyse than previous centuries for a number of reasons. The proximity of the period in question and the vast number of poems available make a clear assessment of major trends very difficult to unravel from this mass of material. Also, the second half of the century, while not immune to fashions in poetry as elsewhere, seems to have been permanently influenced by the 'anything goes' philosophy of the 1960s era. The result is that while the language of poetry generally continues to fluctuate between conformity and revolution, the individual poets are actually free to write in whatever form and style they wish.

As the circular nature of fashions indicates, there are very few really 'new' ideas; most of the time innovations are variations on older themes. The twentieth century has brought with it both recurrent trends, such as the desire to write in everyday language, and apparently new ideas such as free verse. The former was the aim of many generations of poets before the twentieth century and usually arose out of a frustration with 'traditional' poetic language which reflected older modes of speaking. However, the twentieth century has made this regular updating of poetic language more colloquial than, for example, the Romantic poets such as Wordsworth and Coleridge. As well as being more colloquial, the language of twentieth-century poetry has also been more daring in its stretching of the rules of English, whether rules of grammar, semantics or text structure. This experimentation, however, has only in a few cases been different in kind to the type of experimentation which goes on in ordinary conversational contexts. In other words, poets have usually chosen to create meanings in ways which seem natural to speakers of the language.

As mentioned in the previous paragraph, one of the newest and most daring freedoms taken by poetry in the second half of the century is to completely dispense with poetic form. This does not mean that no poet ever uses a strict metre or rhyme scheme; the freedom of the late twentieth century means that you can choose as strict a form as you wish – or no form at all. The increasing use of free verse, however, has blurred the edges between clearly-defined genres of earlier times; short stories or short plays may now sometimes differ very little from poetry.

The overwhelming impression of twentieth-century poetry in English is that the language has been pushed further than ever in the search for ever more apt and aesthetically pleasing expression. This book, which could not hope to be exhaustive, is an introduction to this abundant creativity which marks the twentieth century.

A SHORT HISTORY

The history of poetry in the twentieth century could fill many thick volumes. Indeed, there is a very thorough[1] and interesting survey of the subject by David Perkins (1976, 1987) which occupies two volumes of more than 600 pages each. The present short history, much of which owes a debt to Perkins' volumes, is intended as a simplified framework for the linguistically organised chapters which follow.

The Past

In order to understand some of the developments and trends in twentieth-century poetry, we should look back briefly to the poetry (mainly British) which formed the 'tradition' at the start of the century.

From about 1770 to 1850 there was the period of Romantic poetry – and indeed Romantic art generally. The Romantics held a variety of beliefs and opinions but shared a general reaction against the poetry of their predecessors which was classical in style and reflected the objectivity and rationalism of the age. By contrast, Romantic poetry relied heavily on the poet's imagination, was concerned with nature and individual people (as opposed to civilised society) and employed myth, symbol and imagery in its expression. The innovations of Romantic poetry were clearly a poetic reflection of the political changes occurring at the same time. The French Revolution (1789) is perhaps the most obvious example of 'the people' wanting to overthrow the old order and replace it with something better. The major Romantics (Wordsworth, Coleridge, Keats, Shelley, Byron and Blake) shared an interest in the individual and the imagination, as well as having a heroic notion of the function of the poet. In answer to his own question, 'What is a poet?', Wordsworth answers:

> He is a man speaking to men: a man, it is true, endued with more lively sensibility, more enthusiasm and tenderness, who has a greater knowledge of human nature, and a more comprehensive soul, than are supposed to be common among mankind. . . .

The list of the poet's qualities continues for another fifteen lines, enumerating those areas of thought and expression where a poet excels compared to ordinary people. But the Romantics take seriously the responsibility of such heightened awareness. They 'do not write for poets alone, but for men'.[2]

About the middle of the nineteenth century, the Romantic era of poetry gave way to a more 'Victorian' outlook. The British

Victorians are typically represented by Tennyson, Browning and Barrett-Browning and later by others who were concerned to keep up the 'great tradition' as they saw it. Probably the most obvious characteristic of Victorian poetry is the belief in the rational mind of human beings and a concern with the resulting debates of the day: progress, religious doubt, social responsibility. Tennyson's *In Memoriam*, for example, although a personal poem mourning the loss of a dear friend, is packed with references to contemporary controversial issues. The following lines sum up the religious uncertainty of the times:

> I stretch lame hands of faith, and grope
> And gather dust and chaff, and call
> To what I feel is Lord of all
> And faintly trust the larger hope.

Just before the twentieth century dawned, the avant-garde movement previewed many of the features of the modernism to come. They rejected the Victorian tradition, and adopted 'art for art's sake' as their basic creed, as explained by Perkins (1976):

> *l'art pour l'art* was grounded in hostility to the middle class, its way of life and values . . . it was directed against those writers, chiefly novelists, who held that the purpose of art is a faithful and detailed representation of contemporary and ordinary life.
>
> (p. 34)

The result of this opposition was a belief in the craft of writing: style was everything.

The Twentieth Century Begins

The opening of the century found British poetry reacting to the avant-garde. This poetry is usually called 'Georgian'. The Georgian poets were, as often happens, rejecting their immediate predecessors (the avant-garde) and even those prior to the avant-garde, the Victorians. Instead, the Georgians looked back to the Romantic era as the source of their particular tradition. Their realism was not social as it was in hovels, or psychological as the modernists would make it – but like the Romantics, they were concerned with nature and basic human emotions, especially in connection with the lower social classes. Like Wordsworth, the Georgians expected to find more genuine emotion among the poor than among the rich. An excerpt from *The Owl*, by Edward Thomas, illustrates the combination of nature, emotion and concern for the poor:

> And salted was my food, and my repose,
> Salted and sobered, too, by the bird's voice
> Speaking for all who lay under the stars,
> Soldiers and poor, unable to rejoice.

Later decades derided Georgian poetry for being technically poor and superficial in meaning, but this was partly because modernism had become the new orthodoxy and allowed no opponents. The Georgian poets also suffered from being out of step with their time. The Romantics were part of a general movement in the arts and the sciences which put the natural world at the centre. This was not true of the early part of the twentieth century. The most successful Georgian poet, Robert Frost, expresses this conflict as part of his poetry; being Romantic but rejecting Romanticism. His down-to-earth attitude to life emerges in the light-hearted poem, *Mending Wall*, when he ridicules his neighbour for relying too heavily on walls and fences to keep their relationship sweet:

> Before I built a wall I'd ask to know
> What I was walling in or walling out, . . .
> (ll. 32–3)

Although Robert Frost, a Georgian, was American, the turn of the century in most of America saw the first signs of a modern poetry, which was not yet 'modernist' since it was still very accessible to the average reader. There was also a strong tendency among American poets early in the century to express their Americanism in order to distinguish themselves from the English tradition.

Nationalism of a more urgent kind was prevalent in the poetry of Ireland at this time. Yeats was the most prominent writer to express the fierce and defensive nationalism of a country under siege from a powerful neighbour. The Irish writers of the early years saw themselves as continuing the Celtic revival which had begun in the late nineteenth century, and folklore and myth formed part of the poetic resources of these writers. Yeats's poems, *The Song of Wandering Aengus*, *Fergus and the Druid* and *Cuchulain's Fight with the Sea* are examples of this phase of Irish poetry.

The First World War

The First World War was the turning point for many poets including Wilfred Owen, Rupert Brooke and Siegfried Sassoon. Some of the most famous of the war poets started their writing as Georgians, but by the end of the war their experiences meant that they could no longer write poetry which simply celebrated the natural world and was written for beauty and solace. As Perkins (1976) comments:

> The War Poets were perhaps too close to their subject, but they widened the possible tones and subjects of poetry, and it has never been the same since.
>
> (p. 142)

Wilfred Owen's poetry most clearly illustrates the shocking images which the poets of the First World War were trying to convey. The famous lines from *Dulce et Decorum Est* describing a soldier dying from gas poisoning are typical:

> Dim, through the misty panes and thick green light,
> As under a green sea, I saw him drowning . . .

While the theme was always the same – the brutality of war – the very fact of having written poetry about a man dying of gas poisoning meant that other real-life subjects were also available for poetic treatment.

Modernism

Modernism was not, of course, confined to poetry, but like the Romantic movement over 100 years before, pervaded the arts generally. Poetically the beginnings of modernism can be traced to

the publication of *The Waste Land* in 1922, although others had
published modernist works at about the same time (Ezra Pound,
Marianne Moore, Edith Sitwell and e. e. cummings among
others). The effects of Eliot's innovations were not spread widely
until some time later; the modernist phase lasted about thirty
years (1920s–1950s) in both England and America.

It is significant that most of the early modernists had to train
themselves with some difficulty to write in the particular anti-
popular and esoteric manner that they required. It was not easy to
react against the long-standing views of the function of poetry
typical of the early twentieth century:

> Unless one grasps how generally in the opening years of
> this century it was assumed that poetry is uplifting, solacing
> beauty, one cannot fully appreciate the counter-tendencies.
> Yeats, Brooke, Owen, Eliot, and many other poets trained
> themselves not to write in this way only by effort.
>
> (Perkins, 1976 p. 140)

The new hopelessness which modernism represented can be seen
in the last section of *The Waste Land*, *What the Thunder Said*:

> Here is no water but only rock
> Rock and no water and the sandy road . . .

Not all of the poets mentioned above were modernists (Brooke,
for example, was one of the Georgian poets), but they all fought
against what Brooke called 'unimportant prettiness'.

Some of the other threads which connect the otherwise
rather different modernist poets are the following. The emerging sciences of anthropology and psychology were highly
influential on modernist thinking. The discoveries of the
importance of mythology to the 'primitive' as well as the culti-
vated mind, the unconscious and the workings of the consciousness, the significance of dreams and so on gave poets
new material and suggested new methods of writing. Eliot
explores some of these themes in the *Ash-Wednesday* sequence.
In the following lines he tries to characterise the nature of human
life in relation to death and birth (both literal and spiritual) and
he uses dream imagery:

This is the time of tension between dying and birth
The place of solitude where three dreams cross . . .

(pp. 20–1)

Once again at this period poetry was under increasing pressure
to use more boldly than ever the language spoken by women and
men. This meant not simply freeing grammatical structure from
the constraints of metre and form, but using genuine colloquial
language and rejecting the poetic 'diction' of the last century. The
subjects of poetry were also widened to include the less palatable
emotions and events of the post-War world. The poetry of the
beautiful and pleasing was beginning to lose ground to modern
poetry in the 1920s.

The Thirties

The 1930s saw a reaction against the stronghold of modernism,
with many talented poets, in Britain particularly, rejecting the
exclusive and difficult nature of modernist poetry. Some of the
underlying beliefs of the modernists, for example their faith in
older elitist regimes, were particularly unacceptable to the young
left-wing and idealistic poets who were emerging at the time.
W.H. Auden, Stephen Spender, Louis MacNeice and C. Day
Lewis were among those who were witnessing economic collapse
at home, the rise of fascism in Italy and Germany and the threat
of the Second World War. The horrors of the Spanish Civil War
motivated many young Englishmen to go and fight against the
growing evil of fascism. John Cornford was among those poets
who went to Spain and died there. Others included Christopher
Caudwell and Julian Bell. MacNeice's poem, *Autumn Journal*
(part VI) records the memory of visiting Spain shortly before the
Civil War and not realising what was about to happen:

Not knowing that our blunt
Ideals would find their whetstones, that our spirit
Would find its frontier on the Spanish front,
    Its body in a rag-tag army.

(ll. 97–100)

But despite the growing opposition to modernism, its influence
was not easily overturned and much of the poetry written in the

Thirties retained features of the modernist style, usually rendering the poems relatively obscure.

The Movement and the New Criticism

In the 1940s and 1950s, there were parallel, although independent, developments in the poetry of Britain and America.

The 1940s in America saw the emergence of a new style of criticism, similar to the close reading called 'explication' which was practised in France. Although it was slow to catch on in the colleges, the New Criticism quickly had an effect on the poetic style of young writers of the time. John Berryman, Robert Lowell, Adrienne Rich and James Merrill were among the poets whose early work bore the hallmarks of having been written with criticism in mind. The following lines from the opening of *New Year's Eve* by Berryman exhibit the close style of this era:

> The grey girl who had not been singing stopped,
> And brave new no-sound blew through the acrid air.

The criticism which influenced the work of these poets was text-based, concerned with the language rather than with the life, experience and political or philosophical ideas of the writer. It also encouraged the reader to make an exhaustive search for multiple interpretations, claiming that poems were better for containing ambiguity. As with so many 'movements' which begin outside the establishment, the New Criticism had become the accepted norm of academic study of poetry by the 1950s. Although later trends criticised this phase as being too self-conscious and formal, it did have the virtue of perceiving form and meaning as inseparable. This principle has lasted until the 1990s.

The 1950s in Britain witnessed a reaction against the romanticism of the war years and this was the decade when a group of poets usually grouped under the title 'The Movement' first became well known. Kingsley Amis, Elizabeth Jennings, Philip Larkin, Donald Davie and Thom Gunn, among others, were concerned with representing values opposed to those they saw in '30s and '40s poetry. They therefore reverted to a rational, realistic and sceptical style worthy of the classical tradition of English poetry and they viewed the modernism of Pound and Eliot as foreign and irrelevant. As a result of the Movement's rejection of both mysticism and politics, the subject-matter of much Movement poetry tended to be the ordinary daily facts of life. The style of this poetry, like that of the New Criticism, was carefully crafted and self-conscious of the close scrutiny of texts made by contemporary students, but unlike its American counterpart was direct and uncomplicated. Philip Larkin was one of the best exponents of this style. His concern with everyday matters is well illustrated by some lines from *Mr Bleaney*:

> Flowered curtains, thin and frayed,
> Fall to within five inches of the sill . . .

Beat and Underground Poetry (1950s and '60s)

In the 1950s in America there were a number of related challenges to the impersonal, academic poetry of the New Criticism. The most famous challenge was mounted by the Beat poets, such as Allen Ginsberg and Lawrence Ferlinghetti. Ginsberg's frank treatment in *Howl* (1956) of drug-taking, homosexuality and other features of alternative lifestyles was thoroughly shocking to the poetic establishment of the time. He even dares to be irreverent about one of the poetic heroes of America:

> I saw you, Walt Whitman, childless, lonely old
>   grubber,
> poking away among the meats in the refrigerator
>   and eyeing the grocery boys.

Another departure for the Beat poets was an emphasis on performance, reflecting the feeling that poetry in books had become out-of-touch with the real world and with real people. The Beat poets influenced other trends reacting against the New Criticism. These included 'Confessional' poetry which was also shocking in its subject-matter, but tended to take up personally revealing issues like hate for a father (e.g. Robert Lowell, *Life Studies*, 1959) and Surrealist poetry which belatedly explored some of the Dadaist ideas of early twentieth-century Europe.

The influence of the Beat poets was felt very strongly in the

1960s in Britain. There was a flowering of poetry magazines as well as poetry readings, performances and workshops. The Underground poets were the British equivalent of the Beats and included Michael Horovitz, Adrian Mitchell, Edwin Morgan and Gael Turnbull. These poets rejected the Movement, which they saw as university-based and elitist, and were passionately concerned to take poetry to places where it had not been before. As a result, poetry largely came 'off the page', into performance, and was often associated with the jazz scene which was expanding fast at the same time and provided occasions and venues for poetry reading. The spirit of the Underground years is captured by Michael Horovitz in the 'Afterwords' to his anthology of underground poetry (Horovitz, 1969):

> The stylized accomplishments which make 'selling lines' 'readable' leave them correspondingly 'un-readoutable'. . . . & books – however beautiful – are more and more distant branches, and not the roots of culture communication.

There was, therefore, a postmodernist concern to bring poetry 'to the people' and many poetry societies were set up all over England to host live readings by well-known as well as not so well-known poets. In addition to developing a relationship with jazz, some poetry was used alongside rock music and became closely connected with youth-culture. The Liverpool poets (Roger McGough, Adrian Henri and Brian Patten) are perhaps the most famous example of this phenomenon. They wrote in a spoken style which also reflected their local dialect. They also wrote about things that 'ordinary' people could relate to, such as what it is like on your first day at school, illness or current affairs (Roger McGough's *First Day at School, War of the Roses* and *The Commission* respectively). Adrian Henri, like the other performance poets, uses humour and references to contemporary culture, such as television characters or advertising campaigns in order to make contact with his audience, as in this extract from his poem, *BatPoem*:

> Help us out in Vietnam
>   Batman
> Help us drop that BatNapalm
>   Batman

> Help us drop those jungle towns
> Spreading pain and death around
> Coke'n' Candy wins them round
>   Batman . . .

The belief that poetry should be accessible to all and not elitist and obscure was both a reaction against the academic image of British poetry prior to the 1960s and a reflection of the mood of the decade when popular culture was elevated above traditional arts. The political optimism in Britain allowed for more free expression than ever before, opening up even taboo areas and modern technologies as legitimate subject-matter for poetry. As a result, Marge Piercy was later able to write about rape in *Rape Poem*:

> Fear of rape is a cold wind blowing
> all of the time on a woman's hunched back . . .

And Erica Jong could happily use references to technical household equipment to characterise her mother's life in *Woman Enough*:

> Because my mother's minutes
> were sucked into the roar
> of the vacuum cleaner . . .

Concrete Poetry

One of the experimental phases of the 1960s resulted in what is known as 'concrete poetry'. Its main concern was to experiment with space and visual effects as widely as poetry has always experimented with sound effects. This was a challenge to orthodoxy, like Beat and Underground poetry, but it took a different direction from the performance emphasis of these movements.

Canadian poets such as bp Nichol and bill bissett took up the challenge of concrete poetry, although they later also became performance poets. Nichol in particular took to extremes the use of individual letters in their own right, rather than only using letters as parts of larger units (words). Take, for example, the opening of his poem *Against explanation*:

```
oh the a be
an or and and
c . . .
```

bill bissett developed his own form of spelling which partly reflects the spoken English of Canada. The following example is from: *th wundrfulness uv th mountees our secret police*:

```
they tore my daughtrs dolls hed off
looking for dope . . .
```

It is noticeable that although the most bizarre forms of concrete poetry have long since died away in all but a few places, there remains in more recent poetry a subtlety of spatial awareness that was unknown before the rise of concrete experimentation. In many late twentieth-century Canadian writers, the 'larger-than-usual space' within a line of poetry is just one of these inheritances and can be seen, for example, in *The Conception of Winter* by Claire Harris:

```
                          the moon thin
        a mere slice    diminishing
                             the valley
          the river also diminished
                 the trees    skeletal
                     . . .
```

THE AFRO-CARIBBEAN TRADITION

There are three connected parts of the world where a tradition of poetry in the English language has arisen as a result of British colonialism and the slave trade. These are Africa, the southern States of America and the Caribbean. Since many of the slaves brought to the Caribbean and the southern States were from West Africa, they brought with them traditions and folklore which survived the switch from their own languages to the language of the slave-owners: English. There was, however, also a surprising dependence, particularly in the nineteenth century, on the traditions of English poetry and European styles of poetry generally. This was probably because the literary experience of educated people was almost completely European and even ex-slaves looked up to such models of achievement as the heights to which they should aspire. Another influence was the church, which succeeded in converting many of the slaves to Christianity. Thus even before emancipation in 1807, the slave community, largely illiterate, had oral models of English 'poetry' in the hymns that they learned by heart. Some of the earliest poetry available written by slaves and ex-slaves has the rhythm and even some of the phraseology of traditional English hymns.

The twentieth century, however, has seen an increasing awareness of the importance of black traditions and a willingness to treat seriously the oral songs and poems which had previously been seen as nothing more than the light-hearted entertainment of the oppressed and ignorant black community.

Many of the features of the oral tradition have both survived in Africa and been transplanted to the Caribbean and America. Even later some of these traditions reached Britain as a result of the immigration which Louise Bennett (a Jamaican poet) calls 'Colonization in Reverse'.

The call-and-response song, called 'jamma' or 'work-song' has adapted from the yam fields of Africa to the sugar plantations of slave-worked Caribbean islands and even became a common form of worship alongside more traditional hymns in black communities converted to Christianity in the nineteenth century. A recent example of this form being used in poetry comes from Bruce St John's *Bajan Litany*:

> Follow pattern kill Cadogan   Yes, Lord
> America got black power?   O Lord
> We got black power   Yes, Lord
> . . .

The rest of the poem explores the Barbadian proverb of the first line which warns that mindlessly copying others can lead to disaster.

The African tradition included wide use of satire and this also translated well to the slave-plantations where the owners came in for much ridicule from the slaves in their songs. Since many of the songs used traditionally were intended to be topical, there has always been a great respect for people who can improvise. This particular tradition has seen a resurgence of interest in the 1970s and 1980s with the development of 'dub' poetry where DJs were admired for their ability to invent witty and often politically astute verses to the accompaniment of instrumental music. Dub poetry has now developed into a widely practised poetic form, not restricted to the Caribbean and practised by poets often without the original accompaniment.

Poetry written in English in these three closely connected regions has developed away from a subservient, insecure reliance on the literary traditions of the dominant community, towards the use of local vernacular forms of English. The strong survival of oral traditions in popular entertainment helped because there were structures and themes available for use even by poets working in the written tradition. The problem was how to change the popular perception of vernacular language as only fit for light verse, Standard English being the appropriate vehicle for serious poetry.

In the Caribbean, Louise Bennett (born 1919 in Jamaica) has been the most successful in bringing respectability to the vernacular. She collected folklore from all areas of Jamaica and has written and performed her poetry all over the world as well as lecturing and speaking in many countries. By the 1980s it could be said that 'there is no major poet of the English-speaking Caribbean who does not have the vernacular as one of the languages of his poetry' (Burnett, 1986).

From the 1970s, 'dub' poetry, whose origins are described above, has crossed the boundaries of nation and colour to become popular throughout the English-speaking world. The division between the oral and written traditions has also been successfully blurred in this period, with dub poets publishing and recording their works and black poets generally considering the performance of poetry as an important part of the communication process. This energy and interest in poetic composition parallels the period of Beat and Underground poetry in the 1960s which was mainly a white (and primarily male) phenomenon.

In Africa generally, literature has been slower to react against the European traditions as cultural imperialism and there has been a long-running debate about the de-colonisation of literature, including poetry. In a book on this subject, Chinweizu, Onwuchekwa Jemie and Ihechukwu Madubuike (Chinweizu et al., 1985) confront those that they feel have betrayed the African cause. In the extract below, they are arguing that the nursery rhyme Humpty Dumpty should be valued as not only a simple poem, but also a profound one. For this they were criticised by Wole Soyinka, one of the most successful writers to emerge from Africa in the twentieth century:

> If we choose to tell the British what is valuable or not in their tradition, why not? . . . After all, the bloody British have been going around the world for centuries, telling other people what they should find good or shameful in their own traditions. They may be long overdue for a dose of their own medicine. But really, we have no intention of wasting our energy instructing the British. We only insist on evaluating things for ourselves, on our own terms, in the light of our own interests and perceptions, and not, like Soyinka, in dancing after the march of British opinions on things.
>
> (pp. 245–6)

This extract illustrates the strength of feeling in Africa against joining the European traditions (particularly those of Britain) in writing. The situation is different to that in the United States and the Caribbean where the descendants of slaves are obliged to live in a largely English-speaking world. Independent Africa has the chance to create an identity of its own, albeit largely through the language introduced by the colonialists. Chinweizu et al. observe three groups of poets working from Africa in the middle years of the century (1950–75): the Euromodernists including Soyinka, J.P. Clark and early Christopher Okigbo; the traditionalists including Mazisi Kunene, Kofi Anwoonor, Okot p'Bitek and later Okigbo; and the individualists of the middle ground who share no obvious characteristics, including Gabriel Okara, Lenrie Peters and Dennis Brutus.

While some writers stress the need to break free from Anglo-European traditions, others are more concerned to emphasise the political commitment needed by African writers and are more optimistic about African writers' ability to subvert the language that used to dominate them. Kali Uka, for example, in a paper called *From Commitment to Essence* (Nwoga, 1978), claims that despite the chosen language of writers such as Soyinka and

Achebe being English, they have interwoven African themes and linguistic nuances in a subtle and evolving way:

> A bilingualism then exists. It enhances the transmissions of ideas, the discovery of new expressiveness, new modes. It does not simplify things; it does tell us that a welding together of English and the vernacular, be it Ijaw, Igbo or Yoruba, which can make sense to at least a secondary school leaver, has emerged.

(p. 27)

WOMEN AND FEMINISM

The feminist movement has experienced a similar debate to that of black writers of English literature. The question that remains largely unsolved is whether the 'new' language called for by some theorists as a reaction against the language of the oppressor (i.e. patriarchal English) is too obscure for all but the most intellectual reader.

Throughout the twentieth century the women's movement has progressively changed the relationship between women and poetry. However, the barriers to recognition of women poets, created by white male dominance, remain strong. As Louise Bernikow says in the Introduction to her anthology of women's poetry from 1552 to 1950 (1979):

> 'fame' will continue to be the reward for conformity to class values and a tribute to the skill with which she embodies those values in art.

(p. 5)

The later part of the century has seen much debate in feminist circles about the direction that women's poetry should take. Adrienne Rich addresses this topic, specifically suggesting that language is the key, in her book, *The Dream of a Common Language* (1978). There have been attempts to achieve freedom from the male-oriented language we all speak through creative word-formation and syntax. There have also been attempts, such as Bernikow's anthology (1979) mentioned above, to rediscover women poets and female traditions which have been ignored until recently. And there have been explorations of topics previously seen as unsuitable for poetic subject-matter, such as women's bodily experiences in sex (both heterosexual and lesbian) and childbirth. Adrienne Rich's *Transcendental Etude* is just one possible illustration:

> the homesickness for a woman, for ourselves
> for that acute joy her head and arms
> cast on a wall . . .

However, as Bernikow points out, there is a danger of women's poetry being marginalised as a result of its daring subject-matter:

> Women's lives bore men. The reality of those lives, especially the embarrassing subject of women's bodies, frightens men. Male approval, the condition of a poet's survival, is withheld when a woman shapes her poetry from the very material that contradicts and threatens male reality.
> (p. 7)

The popularising of poetry throughout Britain and North America in the 1960s made little impression upon the relationship of women to poetry. Although anthologies of poetry through the ages have usually included a small minority of women poets, and many women poets have been writing although they have had their work largely ignored, poetry has really not belonged to women until the last three decades of the twentieth century. Even so, a recent mainstream anthology of poetry remains firmly in the tradition of 'male as norm', featuring the work of only five women as compared to fifteen men (Morrison and Motion, 1982).

Although progress measured in such terms has been slow, women's poetry has, in fact, flowered in the last quarter of the twentieth century. Partly as a result of technological innovation, many small publishing houses were set up, some of them exclusively concerned with publishing women's work (e.g. Virago Press, The Women's Press). About twenty years after poetry's popular heyday, women's poetry is expressing solidarity, exploring women's lives and thriving as part of the grass-roots culture of the 'other' half of humanity.

2 The Influence of the Spoken Language

The various rebellions of the twentieth century sketched out in the short history in chapter 1 have given poets the freedom to try representing their own speech, and that of their communities, without worrying about using Standard English or 'acceptable' spelling conventions. It would be wise at this point to consider the nature and definition of Standard English. It is very easy to make simplistic equations between, for example, Standard English and 'The Queen's English' or 'BBC English' but the picture worldwide is more complicated than this.

Standard English evolved from a variety of English previously called the east midland dialect. There are usually four stages in the establishment of a standard language.[1] Firstly one dialect is chosen, secondly it has to be accepted by the powerful ruling and educated classes, thirdly its functions are extended to all the prestigious functions of education and government, and finally there are attempts to make the variety regular in its patterns and as stable as possible. Although this sounds like a deliberate and self-conscious process, in fact it may occur over a long period of time and be only partly engineered by the people it advantages most. In the case of English, it was the dramatic increase in printing following Caxton's introduction of the press in the fifteenth century that gave rise to the need for a stable variety in which to write books for wide circulation. Until the sixteenth century there had been very little cause to worry about the diversity of English varieties because travel was much more restricted and nationwide communication was unknown. Neither was there much concern about the language changing, as almost all linguistic events were

22

ephemeral (even, for example, private letters) and change was therefore imperceptible on a day-to-day basis. Once the east midland dialect had been chosen and accepted as the standard variety it gradually replaced the official and legal functions that had formerly been fulfilled by Latin and French. The eighteenth century (and to some extent also the nineteenth century) saw the greatest conscious attempts to regularise the language and slow down its rate of change. This was the period of prescriptive grammar books and the creation of Samuel Johnson's English dictionary in 1755.

It is clear from the history of Standard English that although it is just another variety of English, equivalent in linguistic terms to any other dialect, it has the status and power associated with the higher classes of British society. While all schoolchildren in Britain and Northern Ireland are encouraged to learn to read and write Standard English, it is not the natural dialect of many children in regions distant from the seat of power in London and the South-East and is the second language of many children in the Celtic countries as well as children of immigrant families. There is, therefore, a disadvantage felt by some regional dialect speakers in trying to use Standard English in educational and employment contexts.

The situation worldwide is similar to that pertaining in Britain, although the complex class structure of English society is not found in other English-speaking countries. The oppression exerted by Standard English in these parts of the world is a colonial one; English arrived in West Africa, South Africa, India, the Caribbean, North America as the language of the invaders and subsequently the rulers of these areas. It was, of course, also the language of slave-owners and slave-traders.

It is not surprising, then, that creative writers should first of all have been constrained to write in the more prestigious dialect and subsequently have felt restricted by the strait-jacket of the standard language, wishing to express themselves in a variety that comes more naturally to them. This desire has only been fulfilled in this century when many (but not all) of the structures and attitudes of oppression were being dismantled. Ironically, many of the early poems written by slaves copied very closely the language and form of the European poetry they had been taught to revere as superior. The following example comes from a poem called *The Poet's Feeble Petition* by George Moses Horton (1797–1883) who taught himself to read by learning the methodist hymnal by heart and comparing the words with those in a spelling book:[2]

> Bewailing mid the ruthless wave,
>   I lift my feeble hand to thee.
> Let me no longer live a slave
>   But drop these fetters and be free.

Although this is a protest poem, it reflects very clearly the language of his oppressors, almost sounding like a hymn itself. If we compare this with something written in the late twentieth century, we can see how much more freely poets now use non-standard varieties of the language. These lines are from *Slave Song* by David Dabydeen:

> Tie me haan up.
> Juk out me eye.
> Haal me teet out
> So me na go bite.
> Put chain rung me neck.
> Lash me foot tight.
> Set yu daag fo gyaad
> Maan til nite – . . .

The freedom to use a familiar variety of English is most important to groups who have been politically oppressed and who often view language as one of the tools of oppression. We have already seen that the women's movement has produced poetry which experiments with language, but of course there is no one dialect common to women since they also belong to other speech communities, such as Yorkshire, the West Indies, New York or Ireland. The whole of this book is about experimentation with language, some of it politically motivated, all of it aesthetically aware. The present chapter, however, aims to describe the ways in which non-standard varieties (rather than unique experiments) have appeared in poetry written in English in the twentieth century. Although all of the poetry being discussed here is written, we could see the spread of non-standard English in poetry as an influence from the speech habits of people who can usually also command the standard variety in the appropriate (usually written) contexts.

The spoken language can influence poetry in a number of ways. Firstly, as we have seen, it may result in the use of a regional dialect. Secondly, there are differences between the spoken and written media, such as minor sentences, which can be carried over into poetic structure. Thirdly, the written language tends to represent a more formal style than the spoken language and poets may also decide to transfer the informality of the spoken style into their work. Although there are vocabulary items at the informal end of the spectrum which are also regionally specific, it is often the case in these days of mass media and communication that informal, slang, product words and so on are common to spoken varieties at least within political boundaries and often throughout the English-speaking world. Since there is some overlap between the three situations described above, the following sections use a structure similar to the book as a whole, looking first at the sounds of language, then at word-formation and word-choice and finally investigating examples of non-standard grammatical structures.

SOUNDS WRITTEN DOWN

Although a detailed exploration of poetry written in dialect belongs in a more specialised volume, we should take note here that there have been more conscious attempts to represent the spoken sounds of dialects of English in the late twentieth century than before.[3] In some cases, there are simple spelling changes to convey a casual spoken style: *Since* **mi** *mam dropped dead* **mi** *dad's took fright.* This example from *Next Door* by Tony Harrison gives the reader a feeling that the poet is chatting to us as a friend. We 'hear' the pronunciation of *my* in a way that we would not if faced with the ordinary spelling. Harrison also indicates features of his parents' accents when he includes quotations such as the following: *It won't be long before Ah'm t'only white!* The representation of *I* by *Ah* gives the reader an idea of the open vowels used by speakers in Leeds where other speakers may use diphthongs. Harrison also shows the common reduction in Yorkshire accents of the definite article to an alveolar plosive, /t/. In fact, the pronunciation of this reduced definite article in Leeds is very often a glottal stop rather than an alveolar plosive, but Harrison is restricted to using symbols that his audience will understand, the relatively unfamiliar symbol for a glottal stop being [?].

Other examples of departures from standard orthography are more extreme. Black poets in the West Indies, Africa, America and Britain have experimented with writing poetry in their pidgin or creole languages based on English. Some of these languages have standardised spellings and some do not. But the lack of a spelling system does not inhibit poets who want to write in their own language. Louise Bennett, who was born and lived in Jamaica, offers a flavour of the local dialect in her poetry:

> **Wat** a joyful news Miss Mattie
> I feel like me heart **gwine burs**
> Jamaica people **colonizin**
> Englan in **revers** . . .
>   (Bennett, *Colonization in Reverse*)

We can see from this extract that certain features of spoken varieties are common to dialects as unrelated as Jamaican Creole and Yorkshire English. The tendency for speakers in both varieties to pronounce the word 'my' with a shortened vowel, /[ɪ]/, instead of the diphthong /ai/ which is inferred from the standard spelling, is represented by the spellings 'me' and 'mi' respectively.

Linton Kwesi Johnson, from Jamaica but educated in London, uses a more radical spelling system which has arisen among the West Indian community partly as a result of increased written use of the creole:

> yu nevah ad noh life fi live
> jus di wan life fi give . . .
>   (Johnson, *Reggae fi Dada*)

There is an attempt here to show the different vowel sounds used by speakers of creole. Since the writers are restricted to using the 26-letter alphabet, conventions arise among writers, such as the use of the symbol 'h' to indicate the shortening, and sometimes the gliding of a vowel.

Many poets around the world who write mainly in Standard English, also speak local languages which influence their writing, sometimes in obvious ways and sometimes quite subtly. Kofi Anyidoho, from Ghana, writes mainly in Standard English, although with rhythmic influences from his first language, Ewe. He also brings some of his poems to life by writing in the local form of West African Pidgin English:

'Old De Boy Kodzo
I write you long long tam, I no dey hear from you.
I say me I go write you someting small again' . . .
(from *My Mailman Friend was Here*)

The pronunciations of 'time' as /tam/ and 'something' with a /t/ where many accents have a /[o]/, work with semantic and grammatical features to portray this character's speech. A final example of poetic attempts to represent pronunciation comes from *Bedtime Story* by Barbara Malcom, a black American poet:

Soldiers
haf to be strong, ya can't be strong
if ya stay wake all night
Now here – take ya gun and the
nation's flag – sleep wit it and
dream bout it – you satisfied . . .

Although such indications of accent are regional and ethnic (e.g. *with* becomes *wit*), many would be appropriate for almost any spoken variety of English. It is common, for example, in connected speech, for unstressed first syllables to disappear as in *wake* (*awake*) or *bout* (*about*). However, it is only in the most radical departures from Standard English that such observations on pronunciation are included. Accents based on regions of England, for example, tend to stay within the accepted spelling conventions for, say, Yorkshire English.

WORD-FORMATION AND WORD COMBINATIONS

It will be seen in chapter 4 that the twentieth century has seen much creative use of the word-formation and combination possibilities of English. Some of these inventions reflect the spoken language in a way that is relevant to this chapter.

One poet who draws on the everyday creativity of the spoken language is e.e. cummings:

> love is **more thicker** than forget
> **more thinner** than recall

and in a later verse:

> **less bigger** than the least begin
> **less littler** than forgive . . .

Here, cummings exploits the fact that some common adjectives may occur with either of the possible comparative inflections; a premodifying *more-* or a suffixed *-er*. However, instead of choosing one or other form, he uses both together to emphasise the comparative element. As well as sounding 'wrong', these inventions give the poem a childlike, naïve air since this kind of 'double comparative' is one of the stages some children go through when learning comparison in English. They also occur in the spoken language when adults jokingly give themselves a false air of innocence by 'making mistakes'. This naïvety is appropriate in the context of a poem that tries hopelessly but repeatedly to define love, sometimes using contradictory phrases.

Another example of the kind of creativity that is heard in everyday spoken contexts is the suffix *-ish*, creating an adjective from a noun. Some poets are particularly fond of creating new words in this way; Auden, for example, uses the *-ish* suffix deliberately to echo spontaneous speech:

> Keep us in our station:
> When we get **pound-noteish** . . .
> (*The Geography of the House*)

And in another poem, *On the Circuit*, he comments upon the preceding line by the phrase *How **grahamgreenish!*** Although the *-ish* suffix is often found attached to single words (e.g. 'I'm hungry*ish*'), Auden is emphasising the spontaneity of its use by adding it to compounds (*pound-note*) and multi-word names (*grahamgreen*).

There is clearly no absolute cut-off point between those inventive derivations which reflect the spoken language and those that do not. Many of the examples in chapter 4 may also sound as though they were invented spontaneously. But although many inventions sound very natural and are used for an aesthetic effect, some examples emphasise their inventedness and sound as though someone has just made them up. It is these examples which have echoes of the spoken language.

The final set of examples of word-formation which reflect the spoken language in this way are those using the suffix *-ly* to create adverbs from adjectives. Louis MacNeice, for example, speaks of the houses in *Birmingham* as being **seducingly** *rigged by the builder* and Bernard Gutteridge, in another poem describing the depressing scenes of the 1930s in Britain, called *Home Revisited*, talks of *the saxifrage* in the garden which is described as *rotting* **brownly** *from the centre*. Finally, Stephen Spender uses the same suffix in his poem *Port Bou* which recounts an incident during the Spanish Civil War in which the narrator tries to come to terms with the fighting and killing. A lorry full of soldiers pulls up next to him and he is confronted by the weapons of war, in this case, a war where one side has very little ammunition: *the famished mouths / Of the rusty carbines brush against their trousers / Almost as* **fragilely** *as reeds*. Here, Spender creates an adverb which would be unlikely to enter the language permanently because of the difficulty of pronouncing the two /l/ sounds so close together. However, it is the kind of word that may well be created time and time again in spoken contexts and this repetitive creation of the word together with its inevitably ephemeral nature symbolises well the themes of the poem; the fragility of life and the constant re-invention of war.

The situation with compound words is similar to that for derivations;[4] many of those created by poets are not intended to reflect the spoken language, but some do so quite blatantly. In *Essential Beauty*, a sharply worded poem attacking the false world of advertising, Philip Larkin describes the hoardings which show cats and slippers by the fire and says that they *Reflect none of the* **rained-on** *streets and squares / They dominate outdoors*. The natural sounding compound *rained-on* which gives itself no airs and could have been said by any passer-by in the street concerned, contrasts well with the highly contrived advertising images of *how life should be*.

Other types of compound which sound colloquial and reflect the spoken language include those which try to describe accurately, for example, a colour that falls between two of the most common colour words in English. In *Snake*, for example, D.H. Lawrence uses the phrase **yellow-brown** *slackness* to describe the snake drinking from his water-trough. It is important that he chooses this way of describing the colour of the snake, rather than searching for a rarer, but accurate colour term such as *ochre*. Lawrence's use of the kind of ready-approximation that speakers use in everyday life adds to the reader's feeling of being present at the scene where carefully considered word-choice is not appropriate.

Another example which reflects the way that speakers describe colour spontaneously comes from Grigson's poem *And Forgetful of Europe* where he describes a deep stream in its **Silk-stocking-coloured** *limestone bed*. This compound illustrates another feature of the colloquial end of the range of compounds; they are sometimes ephemeral because they are tied to a particular era. This compound works because at the end of the twentieth century there is a residual memory of what silk stockings looked like. This memory may not last very much longer. The colloquial compound, as in this case, is often made up of two parts, the first part being a phrase (*silk stocking*). Even longer phrases are sometimes compounded together and used as a single word. Their clumsiness makes them sound freshly coined and evokes the spoken language. Two examples from a very short *Carol* by John Short are used to give the setting for the nativity of Christ:

> He was not dropped in **good-for-lambing** weather
> He took no suck when shook buds sing together
> But he is come in **cold-as-workhouse** weather . . .

The anachronistic use of words such as *workhouse*, like the *silk stockings* in the last example, gives the phrase a very definite time reference to the nineteenth and early twentieth centuries and partly for this reason sounds like a quotation from a spoken context.

The final examples in this section are idioms; combinations of words usually having a meaning in addition to their joint literal meaning. Idioms are common in the spoken language and are used quite liberally in poetry in the twentieth century.

Fern Hill, by Dylan Thomas, for example, has a number of familiar phrases, slightly changed to give them a fresh effect: *once below* a time, all the *sun* long, all the *moon* long, happy as the *heart* was long. The use of *sun* and *moon* to replace *day* and *night* emphasises the young boy's natural rhythms, tuned to the movement of the planet rather than the social conventions of bedtime and rising. Replacing *upon* by *below* emphasises the apparent timelessness of childhood which Thomas is celebrating at the beginning of the poem. The familiarity of the basic phrases harmonises well with the general mood of the poem which describes an idyllic childhood of comfort and security combined with freedom to roam within the confines of the farm.

Some writers make the transitory nature of people's speech the subject of their poetry. Anna Adams, for example, writes about her mother-in-law's language in *Unrecorded Speech*:

'All in a lifetime dear,' she says of death.
Her words may be dead language soon;
that's why I write them down.

Here the poet is focusing on the frequently illogical nature of much of our idiomatic language since the mother-in-law's phrase including the word *lifetime* seems to directly contradict what she is talking about, namely *death*.

WORD-CHOICE (DICTION)

Apart from the invention of words, poets are sometimes influenced by the spoken language in their choice of words. The influence may be from a number of different sources. It may, for example, be the choice of a poet to use regionally distinct vocabulary or vocabulary that is clearly colloquial, possibly even slang or taboo. The reasons why poets make such choices are also varied: the desire to escape from a standard language which is seen as oppressive, the wish to use a spoken style for certain characters within poems, the intention to shock by using vocabulary that is not often seen in print and even, conversely, to reduce the shock value of such words by using them.

Although there is the understandable wish to remain comprehensible to a wide English-speaking audience and this has prevented extensive use of dialect, the increase in 'character' poetry, where the writer uses someone else's voice, has led to a corresponding increase in poetry with a dialect 'flavour'. Tony Harrison's use of a local Leeds dialect has been mentioned in connection with the representation of accent in an earlier section. Clearly it is easier to use vocabulary than accent to give the impression of a dialect, because there is no need to alter the spellings of Standard English words. Harrison celebrates his Yorkshire dialect through the character of his father who constantly bemoans the loss of the old life as in this excerpt from *Next Door IV*:

> They've taken over everything, bar t'Co-op –
> Park's gone west, **chitt'lins**, trotters, **dripping baps!**

Harrison uses **chitterlings** (pigs' intestines) and **dripping baps** (flat breadcakes with the fatty juice from beef) to indicate that what his father sees as normal is becoming unheard of. Ironically, although his father blames the immigrant community, the reader's reaction is likely to be that it is not only immigrant communities that would find these things odd nowadays.

While Harrison's father 'steps in' to his poetry for short speeches, there are an increasing number of poets who write whole poems, or poem-sequences through the eyes of a particular character or characters. Anne Stevenson's poem-sequence, *Correspondences*, for example, traces the history of a New England family around the turn of the century. It is made up of a series of poems written in the 'voice' of one or other of the members of the family and evokes a colloquial, but historical, American dialect partly by its choice of words:

> Now that I've been married for almost four weeks,
> **Mama**,
> I'd better drop you and **Papa** dear a line
> **I guess** I'm fine.
> ('A Daughter's Difficulties as a Wife': Mrs Reuben
> Chandler to her mother in New Orleans, ll. 1–3)

Many of the vocabulary choices of poets are, as they always have been, based on the natural geographical context rather than on the particular dialect of the area. Thus Caribbean poets will talk about *lignum vitae trees* (Dennis Scott, *Weaponsong*) or *molasses*, *cane* (Faustin Charles, *Sugar Cane*). Similarly, the Liverpool poets make many references to the streets and familiar locations in and around Merseyside such as *the East Lancs Road* (Adrian Henri, *Without You*) or *the Cavern* (Roger McGough, *Let Me Die a Youngman's Death*). However, it should not be overlooked that such choices of vocabulary are not always incidental; they are often themselves part of the statement being made by the poet. The relevance of sugar cane to many blacks who have never worked in the plantations themselves is that it symbolises the slave trade. The importance of mentioning the North-West is that English regions other than London and the South-East had been largely ignored by politics and the arts until the second part of the twentieth century.

In addition to regionally influenced vocabulary, there is more and more evidence through the twentieth century of the use of colloquial words and phrases, echoing the spoken language. The informality of these vocabulary choices is just one of the ways in which some poets have tried to demystify poetry so that it is accessible to all readers.

The colloquial choices tend to go with the choice of subject matter as in Douglas Dunn's poem *Among the Houses of Terry Street*:

> On the quiet street, Saturday night's fag-packets,
> Balls of fish and chip newspaper, bottles
> Placed neatly on window-sills, beside cats.

In this poem Dunn paints a picture of a depressed housing area in Hull and the lives of the people who live there. The facts of life (e.g. rubbish in the streets) are made more vivid by the use of *fag-packets* to describe the cigarette packets. The vocabulary that would be used in speech by the residents of Terry Street as well as other speakers (*quit the lav*) gives it a realistic flavour. But the placing of these words within a more formal, written style (e.g. *a blank sobriety, unsmiling in the fogs of deflated mirth*) emphasises the social distance between the classes in England and prevents the poem from sounding simply like a quotation from the people in the Street.

Other poets have also used colloquialisms to demystify. Larkin, for example, has a complex reaction to churches and explores his reasons, no longer religious, for wanting to visit them in a poem called *Church Going*. One of the ways he shows that he no longer

has the religious reverence for a church that calls for 'best behaviour' is by the use of slightly derogatory and colloquial phrases
to describe the contents of the church:

>   some brass and stuff
>   Up at the holy end . . .

The informality of *stuff* and *the holy end* instead of more precise
and technical phrases hints at a point Larkin makes later in the
poem; that his interest is not even one of a historian or student
of architecture. It also conveys a lack of reverence which is
confirmed by his standing at the lectern and pronouncing *'Here
Endeth' much more loudly than I'd meant*.

If colloquialisms and informality have been more widespread in
the twentieth century, then the use of taboo language is certainly
a departure from eighteenth- and nineteenth-century decorum.
Poets, like other artists in the twentieth century, have felt that
part of their mission is to debunk the mythology surrounding the
traditional taboo subjects of sex, religion and bodily functions and
at the same time to emphasise the essentially symbolic nature of
language. In other words, it was important for them to use words
normally only acceptable in the spoken language and in certain
contexts (under your breath, not in front of children or 'ladies',
etc.). There has therefore been an increasing occurrence of so-
called taboo words in the century's poetry.

Maxine Kumin's *The Excrement Poem* chooses the unlikely
subject of defecation not simply to shock, but as the symbol of
cyclical life as she cleans out the horses' stables and adds to the
pile of manure. Her final, celebratory line is : *I honor **shit** for
saying: We go on.* This is just one of the milder examples where
the concern for a casual, spoken style leads to the use of words
which are still rarely printed or published.

Patric Cunnae, in his poem *If Russians didn't exist we'd have to
invent them* also uses taboo words and colloquial vocabulary:

>   Russians, who needs 'em?
>   Shoot 'em
>   Bomb the **bastards** I say
>   Won't it be wonderful
>   When Ronnie gets his way?

The context of this poem and the obvious anti-Cold War stance of its writer indicate that this is supposed to be a quotation from someone whose attitudes Cunnae is ridiculing. The blanket use of a term of abuse like *bastards* applied to all Russians is one way in which the poet achieves this aim.

Perhaps the most interesting way in which taboo language has emerged in poetry is among feminist poets, some of whom have participated in the attempts to 'reclaim' words which have been used as terms of abuse although they refer to parts of the female body. Joan Larkin, for example, has a poem called *'Vagina' Sonnet* dealing with the subject of how such words are used and the political implications of their use. She emphasises the arbitrary nature of words by laughing at a *famous poet* who told her *'Vagina's ugly'*, but at the same time shows herself to be affected by this charge as she wistfully ends her poem with the lines:

> a waste of brains – to be concerned about
> this minor issue of my cunt's good name.

Although this poem is ostensibly concerned with a medical or technical word, *vagina*, it is a word that has taken on the taboo associated with its meaning. More importantly, Joan Larkin manages to make an implicit point about the genuine taboo word, *cunt*, by using it unobtrusively at the end of the poem as the 'normal' word to refer to the vagina. The apologetic and insecure attempt to give *vagina* as a word the same dignity as *penis* masks a strong and subversive use of a much more 'shocking' word.

GRAMMAR

Previous sections have illustrated the way in which the spoken language has contributed sounds, words and meaning to modern poetry. Although non-standard grammar is more noticeable than the occasional dialect or slang vocabulary item, poets have not hesitated, particularly in the second half of the century, to use grammar which reflects everyday usage or the cultural background important to the poet.

If we begin by considering the effects of region on grammar, it is clear that to a lesser extent than with the vocabulary, modern poets have felt free to represent spoken versions of English in their work. Some of the regional variations arise in contexts where a pidgin or creole language based on English is spoken. Kofi Anyidoho, whose poem *My Mailman Friend was Here* was quoted earlier, uses grammatical structures typical of West African pidgin. For example, *I go write you someting small again* has a verb phrase form which differs from the Standard English *am going to write* and this is followed by a pronoun (*you*) which in Standard English would be introduced by a preposition, *to*.

Other grammatical diversions from Standard English which reflect the local dialect of the poet or their characters may be representative of a range of urban British dialects. Tony Harrison is well known for using Yorkshire dialect in his poems and we have already seen how he represents local pronunciation and uses local expressions. There are some grammatical effects too, as in this extract from *Long Distance: **Them** sweets you brought me you can have 'em back*. This use of the pronoun instead of the determiner *those* is common to many non-standard dialects of English and has the effect of making Harrison's father seem real. In a poem called *The Locker*, John Lancaster, another poet working in Yorkshire, also uses *them* to indicate local colloquial speech: *The shop from where he'd bought **them** Friday sweets*.

Anna Adams' poem, *Unrecorded Speech*, was mentioned in an earlier section as being concerned with preserving a style of speech that may otherwise pass away leaving no record behind. In addition to colloquialisms and idioms, she uses non-standard grammatical forms which complete the picture of the mother-in-law's speech style: *How was you, that don't interest me, never no more*. These forms either consist of a form of the auxiliary verb not usually occurring with the pronoun concerned or they contain more than one negative form. They are not regionally restricted but form part of many non-standard British dialects.

As we move through the twentieth century there are more and more examples of reduced forms of verbs and pronouns in poetry, indicating a casual, spoken style, though not restricted to any particular regional dialect. In a poem called *Nuclear defence query* published in 1986, for example, Konny Fraser questions the seriousness of available handbooks giving advice on what to do in a nuclear emergency. She writes in a conversational manner, using reduced forms in a number of places:

> **I've** a screwdriver handy
> that fits every door screw . . .

The poem by Patric Cunnae, *If Russians didn't exist we'd have to invent them*, quoted in the last section, also uses many reduced forms of verbs and pronouns: *who needs 'em?*, **Won't** *it be wonderful.* . . . These are related to the examples quoted in the first section on sounds where some spellings, such as *mi* for *my*, indicate the pronunciation of the word in connected speech. Reduced forms are similar to this, but are conventionally seen as grammatical variants because in some cases the reduction is due to more than speed of delivery.

One of the problems with using the grammatical forms of the spoken language is that speech is not grammatical in the way that writing is usually thought to be. Not many of us, for instance, speak in complete sentences. The problem of representing speech while remaining comprehensible to an unknown audience is one that playwrights have grappled with for a long time, but one that poets have only recently tackled. Poetry has been burdened with the responsibility for 'keeping up standards' in language and it has been difficult even in the twentieth century to abandon the idea that poetry is the repository of 'good style', meaning highly formal and elaborate style. However, there have been an increasing number of attempts to use aspects of spoken grammar, not only to make the words more vivacious, but also to create special poetic effects, some of which are described below.

Minor sentences, sentences without a finite verb, are one way that poets vary their grammatical structures. Minor sentences are common in the spoken language but may also occur in the written language. Both of the following examples are from *Canticle for Good Friday* by Geoffrey Hill. The first consists of a noun phrase, not followed by a verb of any kind:

> A clamping cold-figured day

and the second contains subject and complement but no verb to create a full sentence:

> He,
> As yet unsearched,unscratched.

One of the effects of minor sentences is that, lacking a finite verb, there is no tense given. Therefore these sentences can create a kind of timeless atmosphere. In the case of Hill's poem, those watching Jesus die on the cross may well have felt that time stood still, and the structure therefore echoes these feelings. The final section of chapter 7 illustrates more fully this kind of symbolic use of grammar.

The following excerpt from *Downpour* by Penelope Shuttle has two sentences, neither of which includes a main verb, though the first has three participles (*blown*, *seeping* and *helped*) and one finite verb (*comes*) all occurring in subordinate clauses:

> Through the letter box, leaves instead of letters,
> wet leaves blown along the path
> and seeping through the low letter box,
> an invasion that comes slowly,
> but helped by the rain. The downpour.

The effect of avoiding main verbs in this way is again to make the poem timeless, by refusing to anchor the 'action' (or, in this case, 'inaction') in a particular time span.

Sometimes the non-standard structures used by poets to indicate spoken style are repeated and become stylised, giving a sense of form to the poem. Nicki Jackowska, for example, opens some of her poems with the conjunction *and*, a use which is typical of spoken but not written English. The opening line of *Family Outing – A Celebration*, for example, is: *And I took myself for a walk in the woods that day*. The effect is that the readers feel that they are part of a casual conversation, almost as though they were leaning on the garden wall and talking to a neighbour. Although she uses very little punctuation, so we cannot tell immediately where the ends of sentences are, the poet introduces apparently new structures with *and* a number of times later in the same poem. For example: *And I took my wives and daughters, carrying provisions* (l. 5), and later: *And my father, with his stern blue eye* (l. 7). The capital letters indicate a new sentence, although there is no preceding full-stop and these departures from standard punctuation add to the effect of a rather breathless piling up of sentences in a storytelling style.

3 The Sound of Twentieth-Century Poetry

> Man, you must sweat
> And rhyme your guts taut, if you'd build
> Your verse a ladder.
>> (R.S. Thomas, *Poetry for Supper*)

Like the poetry of earlier times, the poetry of the twentieth century sees the sounds of English as one of its most important resources. Many of the techniques used, such as alliteration, metre and rhyme, belong to the tradition of poetry in English, but have been used in new and different ways since the turn of the century. Some techniques, like the spatial and orthographic innovations of concrete poetry and like the increased use of dialect, are products of the greater freedom of composition felt by twentieth-century poets.

POETIC SOUNDS

As well as the new freedom to depart from standard spellings, poets in the twentieth century have had other constraints relaxed. Some of the most rigid of these constraints were the acceptance of regular metre and, in some cases, regular patterns of rhyme or alliteration. The liberty to use any metre or no metre and any combination of sound patterns has had the effect that the traditional terminology for accepted patterns of sound and metre is no longer adequate. Rather than proliferating technical vocabulary to cover all the new sound effects, it makes sense to use existing linguistic vocabulary to describe individual examples in terms of their phonological and prosodic properties. This chapter uses the phonological symbols shown in the 'Guide to Pronunciation' to describe individual sounds and defines metre and rhythm in terms of stressed and unstressed syllables. The most well-known traditional terms, such as 'rhyme' and 'alliteration' are also used when appropriate.

The division into musical and meaningful uses of sound in poetry is, as usual with such divisions, arbitrary. However, it is useful to note that there are some effects of sound which cannot be tied directly to the meaning of the poem; they invite description in words more usually applied to music such as 'bouncy', 'flowing', or 'sonorous'. This aspect of the sound of poetry appeals to the aesthetic sense without necessarily involving the intellect in interpreting its meaning.

MUSICAL USE OF SOUND

Metre and Rhythm

Metre, the regular ordering of syllables into rhythmic patterns, is no longer considered to be a necessary feature of poetry. This change marks the most striking difference of form between poetry of the twentieth century and poetry of previous times. The only noticeable exception to this is in the area of poetry written for children which has remained largely metrical and rhyming until very recently. There are now a few poets who write free verse for children (e.g. Mike Rosen), but even where a poem lacks form, rhythm and internal rhyme are still important to children. Poetry written in English has long been dominated by a small range of metres, primarily iambic pentameter which consists of five 'feet' each containing an unstressed syllable followed by a stressed syllable. It is seen, for example, in the opening lines of Milton's *Samson Agonistes*:

A líttle ónward lénd thy guíding hánd
To these dárk stéps, a líttle fúrther ón . . .

Traditionally, poetry has allowed slight variations in its metre, as seen in the second line above. Here, the opening of two unstressed syllables followed by two stressed syllables makes the reader pause over *dark steps*, which emphasises the fumbling progress of the blind Samson. Before the present century, however, most poems would have an identifiable metric pattern often used in conjunction with a regular rhyme scheme. *The Sunne Rising* by Donne, for example, has three stanzas with the rhyming scheme abbacdcdee and also has the same number of syllables in equivalent lines from each stanza. The ten lines of each stanza contain 8–4–10–10–8–8–10–10–10–10 syllables respectively, although their stressed syllables vary in number and position as seen by comparing the fifth line from stanzas 1 and 2:

> Sáwcy pedántique wrétch, goe chíde
> If her éyes have not blínded thíne . . .

In the twentieth century, poets have felt free to produce poetry ranging from the highly metrical to work which is apparently free of rhythmical structure. Some modern poets use a traditional structure, such as the ballad form, to make a link with the poetic tradition while retaining a 'modern', innovative style in vocabulary or subject matter. The effect of using strict metre in a century when it is not necessarily expected is often comical:

> I ám a yóung exécutive. No cúffs than míne are
>   cléaner;
> I háve a Slímline bríef-case and I úse the fírm's
>   Cortína.

These lines from *The Executive* by John Betjeman illustrate his skill in combining strict metre with modern topics and vocabulary. The amusing and apparently trivial nature of the subject-matter is emphasised by the 'jolly' metre. However, this impression is belied by the emerging unattractive picture of a ruthless property developer:

> I do some mild developing. The sort of place I need
> Is a quiet country market town that's rather run to
>   seed.
> A luncheon and a drink or two, a little savoir faire
> I fix the Planning Officer, the Town Clerk and the
>   Mayor.

The lighthearted appearance of this poem is successfully undermined by understatements such as *mild developing* and aggressive
vocabulary such as *fix*.

A more recent use of fairly rigid metre is found in Rosemary Norman's poem *My son and I*. The second stanza illustrates the rhythm:

> He hás no intentions
> Not évil or góod
> But his téars have a fúnction
> To gét him his fóod.

There are two main stresses in each line, with two unstressed
syllables between them. This unrelenting drumbeat emphasises the
writer's perception of her life looking after a baby as a frustrating
and dull routine. As with the Betjeman poem, it is easy for modern
readers to overlook the seriousness of such poetry, since regular
rhythm is often associated with trivial verse or children's poetry.
The note of panic in the last stanza is, however, difficult to ignore:

> That is less than enough
> As too plainly appears,
> But my will runs to waste
> In incontinent tears.

As the above examples show, the use of metre in twentieth-century
poetry is the free choice of the poet. The effects, therefore, tend to
be symbolic; the 'sing-song' rhythm conceals a darker side to the
executive and the two-beat rhythm in Norman's poem symbolises
the inflexible pattern of feeding and nappy-changing.

Poems with fluctuating rhythms or no metrical shape at all have
become more common through the twentieth century than poems
with strict metre. Although there is great variation within recent
poetry, there seems to have been a decline in the use of metrical
structure; poets writing in the early part of the century often
imposed some metrical form on their poems:

> It séemed that out of báttle I escáped
> Down some profóund dúll túnnel, long since scóoped
> Through gránites which titánic wárs had gróined.
>
> > (ll. 1–3)

Strange Meeting by Wilfred Owen is written in lines which are almost all ten syllables long. The poem is not, however, predictable or banal in its rhythm since the stresses vary in their number and position. This kind of metric pattern is sometimes called 'syllabic' and is considered to be a feature of this century's poetry, particularly represented in the work of Dylan Thomas and Thom Gunn. In their work, the lines usually have a different number of syllables, but the syllabic pattern is repeated in each stanza. *Poem in October* by Thomas, for example, has lines with 9–12–9–3–5–12–12–5–3–9 syllables and this pattern is repeated for each of the seven stanzas. The following is the first stanza:

> It was my thirtieth year to heaven
> Woke to my hearing from harbour and neighbour wood
> And the mussel pooled and the heron
> Priested shore
> The morning beckon
> With water praying and call of seagull and rook
> And the knock of sailing boats on the net webbed wall
> Myself to set foot
> That second
> In the still sleeping town and set forth.

There is an interaction here between the metric pattern and other sound patterns which will be described in later sections of this chapter. The impact of different stress patterns in lines with the same number of syllables is most striking when we compare lines 2 and 7 from the stanza quoted above:

> Wóke to° my° héaring° from° hárbour° and° néigh-
>   bour° wood°
>
> And° the° knóck of° sáiling° boats° on° the° nét
>   wébbed wáll . . .

Line 2 has a rhythmical beat and a regular pattern of one stressed syllable followed by two unstressed syllables, repeated four times. The last syllable, *wood*, would usually be expected to carry a main stress, but the momentum of the pattern within this line carries over, making the word unstressed. This demotion is reinforced by an echo from the word *neighbourhood* whose final syllable is unstressed. In contrast, line 7 has an irregular pattern of stress ending with a string of four unstressed syllables followed by three stressed syllables. The final phrase, *net webbed wall*, echoes the sound of boats knocking against the wall by a combination of alliteration, assonance and stress.

Although free verse (unrhymed, non-metrical poetry) has increased in popularity through the twentieth century, metre (particularly syllabic metre) remains quite usual in poems written up to the present day. *The Lost Continent* by Jenny Joseph, for example, has ten-syllable lines which usually have five main stresses per line, but are not all arranged in an iambic pattern (i.e. with five feet of unstressed + stressed syllable):

> A thréad of sílver márks alóng the sánd
> The shállow stárt of the déep ócean. Drý
> Amóng the dúnes a rústy cáble póints
> Twó fíngers to the whíte and mórning áir.

Many poets, however, impose no such restrictions on the form of their poems. Elaine Feinstein uses metre in some of her poetry, but in *Calliope in the labour ward*, for example, there is no overall pattern. This poem has five stanzas with 2–5–6–4–4 lines respectively and the lines vary between 2 and 12 syllables. The length of the lines is musical, but not in the same way as regular metre is musical. The one 12-syllable line symbolises the gradual onset of a uterine contraction and echoes the sea/tide metaphor used to describe the pain of labour:

> and time opens
> pain in the shallows to wave up and over them . . .

The rhythms used in this poem, therefore, are both symbolic and musical and begin to show the meaningful use of sound. The last stanza is made up of very short lines and is clearly intended to represent the short sharp breaths of the later stages of giving birth:

> in that abandon less
> than human
> give birth
> bleak as a goddess . . .

One of the century's poets who has written almost entirely in free verse is D.H. Lawrence. His most famous animal poem, *Snake*, is written in lines varying from 3 syllables to 20 syllables. A sense of form is retained by repetition of structures and sometimes of complete phrases:

> Was it cowardice, that I dared not kill him?
> Was it perversity, that I longed to talk to him?
> Was it humility, to feel so honoured?
> I felt so honoured.

> (ll. 31–4)

Although the trend in much of the century's poetry has been away from strict form, cultural sub-groups such as women and black poets have sometimes looked for inspiration toward a folk tradition of songs and oral storytelling which they felt would represent their ancestry better than the mainstream tradition of English poetry. Irish poetry went through a similar process of self-discovery around the turn of the century when Yeats, among others, looked to the folk songs of Ireland for his sources.[1] In addition, since the 1960s there has been a close alliance between music and poetry, especially poetry written in opposition to the establishment of the time. The result is that there are a number of clusters of poems which are written in more regular metre and with stricter rhyme schemes than we would expect. The example given here is from *Free Up de Lan, White Man* by Mutabaruka:

> Free up de lan, white man
> free de Namibian
> Free up de lan, white man
> free all African . . .

This 'chorus' occurs between the longer stanzas of the poem which are also regular in metre and rhyme.

Sound Harmony

The ways in which individual sounds contribute to the music of poetry can be generalised as 'harmony' since they all involve similarity of sound at some point in the syllable. Although there is a wide range of harmony in poetry the harmonies can be conveniently divided

into those concerned with consonants (alliteration) or vowels (assonance) or combinations of consonants and vowels (rhyme).

Alliteration is perhaps one of the oldest uses of sound in
poetry as it was used to anchor the sound of Anglo-Saxon poetry.
There have been occasional revivals of this regular alliterative
style, but most poetry in English in all periods has used alliteration sporadically when it was likely to enhance the sound and
sometimes also the meaning of the work. Alliteration in the
twentieth century has three main uses in poetry. It can be used
to produce music by an unusually high density of certain
consonants. It can also be used symbolically to emphasise an
onomatopoeic or sound-symbolic effect. Finally, it can be used
simply to highlight particular words and the meaning relationship
they share.

The term 'alliteration' is usually assumed to refer to closely
placed words beginning with the same consonant as in the following examples from *Thrushes* by Ted Hughes:

> how loud and above what
> **F**urious spaces of **f**ire do the **d**istracting **d**evils
> Orgy and hosannah, under **w**hat **w**ilderness
> Of black silent **w**ater **w**eep.

Although alliteration is mainly seen as part of the harmony of
poetry, many examples also suggest some symbolic association
between the sound and the meaning. The use of the fricative
sound /f/ to represent hellfire is almost onomatopoeic in its
evocation of the spitting flames and is in stark contrast with the
bleak silence evoked by the repetitive use of /w/ which belongs to
the aptly named group of 'liquid' consonants. There will be more
discussion of onomatopoeia and sound-symbolism later in this
chapter, but this example shows that such meaningful effects may
depend on highlighting by alliteration.

As in most periods of literary history, the twentieth century has
produced some poets who delight in the sounds of English
and who use generously all the techniques of harmony available
to them. Dylan Thomas had a gift for weaving intricate
patterns of sound which were musical without sounding contrived.
Some of the many examples of alliteration in *Fern Hill* appear
in this extract:

> And green and golden I was huntsman and herdsman,
>   the calves
> Sang to my horn, the foxes on the hills barked clear
>   and cold . . .

The alliteration which represents the sound of the foxes by repetition of /k/ illustrates the important point that it is the sound, not the spelling, which creates most alliterative effects. Most consonants in English are fairly consistent in their pronunciation, but there are examples where an apparent alliteration will disappear on being read aloud. In Auden's *Moon Landing*, for example, the poet questions the wisdom of space travel in the line: *A grand gesture. But what does it period*? The use of such 'eye-alliteration' is rare, perhaps because poetry seems to invite a mental 'reading' which would soon distinguish the /g/ of *grand* from the /dʒ/ of *gesture*.

Many modern poets extend the scope of alliteration to include the accumulation of similar consonants in syllable-initial and syllable-final positions. The effect is one of increased density of sound as seen in the following line from *The Second Coming* by W.B. Yeats:

> Mere anarchy is loosed upon the world,
> The blood-dimmed tide is loosed, and everywhere
> The ceremony of innocence is drowned; . . .

A different effect is created by the occurrence of a number of consonants from related phonological groups. An example from another poem by Yeats, *Byzantium*, has a number of nasal consonants (/n/ and /m/) and a cross-cutting group of bilabial consonants (/b/ and /m/):

> For Hades' bobbin bound in mummy-cloth
> May unwind the winding path; . . .

Although different readers may infer different symbolic connections from this line, there is a clear musical 'colour' in such a phrase which would sound totally different if the predominant consonants were all velar fricatives or sibilants.

. A final example of alliteration comes from a poem by Philip Larkin and shows how similar consonants are sometimes used to highlight particular relationships between words. In Larkin's poem, the alliteration picks out words which he wishes to present as opposite in meaning. The examples come from lines 3, 5 and 8 respectively:

> Is it a **tr**ick or a **tr**ysting-place,
> Is it a **m**irage or **m**iracle,
> Are they a **s**ham or a **s**ign?

This poem, *XXVII*, addresses the problem of being sure when love is real and everlasting. The oppositions quoted above reveal the poet's insecurity in recognising 'true love'. There is a vertical relationship between the pairs since *trick*, *mirage* and *sham* are partial synonyms sharing an element of deceit in their meaning and *trysting-place* is drawn into another set of partial synonyms with *miracle* and *sign* which have a quality of real magic. The conclusion of the poem is that there is no essential difference between these apparent opposites since everlasting love is simply constructed from an infinite number of moments in the present:

> I take you for now and for always,
> For always is always now.

The alliteration in this poem serves not only to highlight the significant words, but to emphasise the fact that despite their apparent opposition, they are the same.

The poetry of the twentieth century has possibly used alliteration no more and no differently than poetry of previous centuries, but assonance in modern poetry seems to differ in quantity if not in usage and effects. Some poets, represented typically by Dylan Thomas, have indulged in the use of vowel harmony with great relish as the series of /o/ sounds in the following passage from *Fern Hill* illustrates:

> Nothing I cared, in the lamb white days, that time
>   would take me
> Up to the swallow-thronged loft by the shadow of my
>   hand, . . .

Another poet who at times takes an almost childlike delight in sounds is e.e. cummings. His poem which starts *in Just/ spring* (his poems are not named) is written from a child's viewpoint and wallows in the /ʌ/ or /u/ vowel (depending on your accent) when he describes the world as *mud-luscious* and later as *puddle-wonderful*.

Rhyme remains a conspicuous feature of the sound of poetry in English but, as with other sound effects in poetry, poets are not constrained by rules governing the use of rhyme and are therefore free to choose whether and how often to make their verse rhyme. The most obvious type of rhyme holds between two strong syllables which share the same vowel and final consonant cluster:

> I rode with my darling in the dark wood at n**ight**
> And suddenly there was an angel burning br**ight** . . .
> (Stevie Smith, *I rode with my darling*)

The gradual abandoning of strict poetic rules in this century has allowed for an expanded use of other, lesser kinds of rhyme, such as the occurrence of syllables ending with the same consonant cluster but differing in their vowels. The ends of lines in *VI* by Philip Larkin, for example, almost all take part in such imperfect rhymes:

lines	2 & 5 – back/two o'clock	/-k/
lines	7 & 9 – gone/alone	/-n/
lines	8 & 11 – confront/plant	/-nt
lines	10 & 11 – increase/idleness	/-s/

Other effects which are less than full rhymes may include syllables which share both initial and final consonant clusters, such as *miss mass* from Roger McGough's *ofa sunday*:

> miss mass
> and wonder
> if mass misses me . . .

The final example of imperfect rhyme is sometimes called 'reverse rhyme' since it is the initial consonant cluster and the vowel which are similar; the final consonant differs. Although all types of rhyme can occur either at line ends or within the line, reverse rhyme tends to occur more frequently within the line, making an effect similar to, but possibly more prominent than alliteration, as in this line from *Dulce et Decorum Est* by Wilfred Owen: *His hanging face, like a devil's **sick** of **sin***.

It would be impossible in an introductory book to make a comprehensive survey of all the ways in which the sounds and rhythms of English have been used in twentieth-century poetry. It has always been true that the best-remembered poets evolve a style that is their own and this usually includes a music that is a unique blend of the sound effects available. The difference between previous centuries and the twentieth century is that there are now more opportunities for variation than before. As in other aspects of life, the fashion of poetry in the late twentieth century dictates simply that 'anything goes'. A contemporary poet may choose to write in a syllabic metre with end rhymes (e.g. Larkin), in an accentual metre with end rhymes (e.g. Betjeman), in a syllabic metre with no end rhymes but with an abundance of alliteration and assonance (e.g. Dylan Thomas), in a metre-less rhythm with no rhymes but occasional appropriate use of alliteration or assonance (e.g. Sylvia Plath), and some poets experiment with a wide variety of metres and harmonies in different poems (e.g. R.S. Thomas). There are many other possible combinations and very few generalisations that can be made. However, it could be claimed with some accuracy that the perceived obligation to use some kind of metre and/or regular rhyme scheme has diminished significantly since the beginning of the century.

BETWEEN MUSIC AND MEANING

Although it has been useful to separate musical from meaningful uses of sound in poetry, it has already become apparent that there are many examples where the distinction is not appropriate, as exemplified by the fricatives in *Thrushes* by Ted Hughes which symbolise hellfire. The same poem has examples of assonance which are both musically gratifying and potentially symbolic:

> Carving at a tiny ivory ornament
> For years: his act worships itself – while for him,
> Though he bends to be blent in the prayer, how loud
>   and above what
> Furious spaces of fire do the distracting devils . . .

These three pairs of vowels (or diphthongs), /ai/, /e/ and /au/ represent a kind of progression from closed to open vowels. First, the diphthong /ai/ (tiny, ivory), ends with the mouth in a closed position /i/ which symbolises the size of the ornament and the inward-looking nature of human art. Secondly, the vowel /e/ is half-open, but still quite introspective (even its orthographic form suggests a curled-up person) and it emphasises the earnest nature of the task. By contrast, /au/ is a more open diphthong because it consists of back vowels which keep the mouth in a more open position. This diphthong underlines the difference between the act which *worships itself* and the *distracting devils* which pull people away from their determined path.

These examples show that it is often possible to provide explanations for sound effects such as alliteration or tie the metrical form of a poem to its meaning. However, many of the sounds of poetry cannot be objectified in this way and must simply be explained in terms which recognise their musical qualities.

MEANINGFUL USE OF SOUND

The meaningful uses of sound can be divided into two main categories; onomatopoeia and sound-symbolism. These terms have been defined in various ways, but here they are used in the following way.

'Sound-symbolism' means the use of individual or combined sounds to represent a feature of meaning shared by a number of words. For example, the words *slip*, *slide*, *slimy* and *slink* share a feature of meaning which might be described as 'smooth' and which seems to be located in the initial consonant cluster /sl/. They are rather different in other aspects of their meaning. These words are 'conventionally sound-symbolic'; they connote smoothness irrespective of context by a tacit reference to other similar words. Other sets of words may be sound-symbolic only when juxtaposed in a particular setting such as a poem. The words connected by conventional or invented sound-symbolism are not necessarily connected in any other way. *Slink* and *slimy*, for example, are very different in other ways, *slink* being a movement verb and *slimy* a descriptive adjective.

The term 'onomatopoeia' will be used here to refer to a special sub-category of sound-symbolism, when some sounds in a word (or the whole word) echo the sound indicated by the word itself.

Conventional examples are the animal noises such as *moo* and *neigh* and inanimate noises such as *crack* or *thud*. Poets may also create onomatopoeic effects which work only in context.

Onomatopeia

Because of its special status symbolising sound, onomatopoeia has the distinction of being the only aspect of English where there is an intrinsic connection between the language and the 'real world'. It is well known that the connection between words and their referents is arbitrary; *house* is no more appropriate than *maison* (French) or *casa* (Spanish). Onomatopoeic words, however, may have a physical connection with their referents; the sound of wind is created by air moving through a restricted passage and this description is equally valid for the fricative consonants which may be used to represent the wind in a poetic context:

> I lay in an agony of imagination as the wind
> Limped up the stairs and puffed on the landings,
> Snuffled through floorboards from the foundations, . . .
> (P. Redgrove, *Old House*)

The use of conventional onomatopoeia in modern poetry is not remarkable in itself, although it may stand out from the surrounding text, as in *He swallowed, unresisting;* **moaned** *and dropped* or *He dipped contented oars, and* **sighed***, and slept.* These lines from *The Death-Bed* by Siegfried Sassoon use the onomatopoeic words *moaned* and *sighed* in a straightforward way. The parallelism of the structure in these two lines, however, highlights the progression from action (*swallowed*, *dipped*) through involuntary sounds (*moaned*, *sighed*) to insensibility (*dropped*, *slept*). This pattern, as well as pointing out similarities, emphasises the difference in the two events; the first is an uncomfortable blackout to escape from the pain of his wound. The soldier's continued state of semi-consciousness is portrayed in the run-on line:

> and dropped
> through crimson gloom to darkness; . . .

The second sequence of verbs contrasts with the first in its comparative comfort (*contented*) and the end-stopped line suggests that the consciousness has finally allowed both body and mind to rest. The onomatopoeic words, then, form one strand in a complex interweaving of lexical, grammatical and phonological effects.

More unusual uses of conventional onomatopoeia include those where the suggestion of sounds is unexpected:

> The woman in the block of ivory soap
> has massive thighs that **neigh**,
> great breasts that **blare** and strong arms that trumpet.

This extract from *The Woman in the Ordinary* by Marge Piercy uses onomatopoeic words to suggest a figurative connection between parts of the woman's body and certain sounds. The overall effect of these lines is one of enormous strength; her thighs are like great horses, her breasts, perhaps, have the power of high amplitude loudspeakers.

Often the choice of a single onomatopoeic word has an extraordinary power to evoke the sound it conveys. This is true of one of the many effective words in *Dulce et Decorum Est* by Wilfred Owen:

> If you could hear, at every jolt, the blood
> Come **gargling** from the froth-corrupted lungs, . . .

The production of a velar plosive, /g/, sound involves a constriction of the throat similar to the action of gargling and its repetition in the word (possibly three times for some accents of English) reflects the repetitive nature of the sound. The displacement of this word from its more usual setting in the treatment of sore throats is very effective. Owen uses it in the vivid and shocking picture of a dead soldier whose blood causes his throat to make an involuntary gargling noise.

In addition to using conventional onomatopoeia in unusual and effective ways, poets of the twentieth century have created contextual onomatopoeia by exploiting auditory aspects of individual sounds and groups of sounds. One example of the use of plosive sounds is found in this extract from *Canticle for Good Friday* by Geoffrey Hill:

> While the dulled wood
> Spat on the stones each drop
> Of deliberate blood.

The regular dripping of blood is evoked by the plosive sounds which share the phonological property of having a definite onset made by the explosion of air through a closure in the mouth. They are therefore well-suited to evoking the sound of drips which also has a sharply focused onset.

Although there is clearly a shared perception among native speakers about the appropriateness of such use of sound, this cannot be described as conventional since the same effect would not be recognised in these words out of context, when their combined meaning would disappear.

Other groups of sounds are also used to build up an onomatopoeic effect. The soft sound of explosions heard from a distance, for example, is evoked by the onomatopoeic word *hoots* and is echoed by sibilants in these lines from *Dulce et Decorum Est* (Owen):

> deaf even to the hoots
> Of gas shells dropping softly behind.

In her poem *Morning Song*, Sylvia Plath makes effective use of the voiceless fricative, /θ/, to suggest the almost imperceptible breathing of a new baby:

> All night your moth-breath
> Flickers among the flat pink roses.

Sound-symbolism

Poets of earlier times have used sound-symbolism in their work, although we may hypothesise that the decline in metre and rhyme corresponds to a compensating increase in other sound effects, including sound-symbolism.

The English language provides the poet with a wide range of conventional symbolism to which readers respond almost instinctively. The following lines from Marge Piercy's poem *The Woman in the Ordinary* illustrate:

The woman in the ordinary pudgy downcast girl
is **crouching** with eyes and muscles **clenched** . . .

There is a symbolic link here between the /-tʃ/ in *crouch* and in
clench; it represents the tightly bunched-up nature of the position
described by each word. The initial consonant cluster of *clenched*,
/kl-/, also has a separable meaning which may be paraphrased as
'determined not to let go' and is shared by such words as *cling* and
clasp.

Conventional sound-symbolism is most noticeable, as in the last
example, when there are two or more words in a poem carrying
the same symbolic cluster of sounds. Seamus Heaney's poem
Funeral Rites uses another pair of words whose meanings are
partly connected by sound. Describing the faces of dead relatives,
he uses the adjective *glistening* about their eyelids and later talks
of the *gleaming* crosses adorning the nails of the waiting coffin
lids. These words share the initial consonant cluster /gl-/ which
also occurs (though not in the poem) in *glisten* and *glow*. The
shared part of their meaning, 'reflected light', is clearly a vital
feature of the traditional funerals that Heaney is describing and
helps to evoke for the reader the candle-lit interior of the room.

Onomatopoeia has already been described as a special sub-type
of sound-symbolism. There are some interesting examples of
overlap in modern poetry where the boundary between sounds
representing sounds and sounds representing other aspects of
meaning is unclear.

In *Welsh Landscape*, for example, R.S. Thomas extends the
sound-symbolism of the palatal fricative, /ʃ/, in 'hush' over three
words:

And thick ambu**sh** of **sh**adows,
Hu**sh**ed at the fields' corners . . .

This use of 'sh' to represent silence is, of course, conventional. It
does not, however, imitate silence since the very uttering of the
sound disrupts any silence there may have been.

Other kinds of connection between onomatopoeia and sound-
symbolism can be illustrated by examples from *Broadcast* by Philip
Larkin. The setting is a concert hall and the drum roll which calls
the attention of the audience is described as *a sudden* **scuttle** *on the*

drum. The word *scuttle* conventionally refers to the movement of small mammals and additionally connotes the sound of their nails on the floor. Both aspects of the word's meaning are carried over to Larkin's context, but with their priorities reversed. In the case of the drum, the sound (which shares some aspects of its ono-matopoeiac effects with other sound words such as *rattle*) is primary but the movement of drumsticks across the skin is also evoked.

Larkin uses another onomatopoeic word, *snivel*, to describe the sound of violins tuning before the concert. This word is usually associated with a nasty kind of child's crying which has a nasal sound symbolised by the initial consonant cluster /sn-/. This cluster also symbolises the 'nasty' element of the word's meaning as shared by non-sound words such as *snide*, *sneer*, *sneaky* and *snoop*. Its use to describe the unpleasant, whining sound of violins being tuned is very effective.

4 Word Forms and Combinations

WORD-FORMATION

> Twas brillig and the slithy toves
> Did gyre and gimble in the wabe . . .

When we think of the invention of words, neologisms like those in Lewis Carroll's *Jabberwocky* spring to mind. Many of his inventions are simply made up of sequences of sounds which are acceptable in English, but which apparently have no specific meaning for English speakers. Of course, if this were so, the reader would have little hope of understanding the poetry. In fact, as discussed in chapter 3, many sound-symbolic sequences which have no reference to the real world may still have meaning for English speakers. Thus the /br-/ consonant cluster at the beginning of *brillig* reminds us of *bright* and *brilliant*, the /sl / cluster in *slithy* recalls the unpleasant smoothness of *slimy*, *slither* and *slippery* and the /-mbl/ ending of *gimble* implies something of the relaxed nature of words like *gambol*, *tumble* and *amble*.

In this section, however, we are concerned with words whose meaning is carried not by sounds, but by its constituent parts (existing English words and morphemes). These words are created from units, and by processes which already have consistent meaning in English. Word-formation in the poetry of the twentieth century reflects the creative processes which are in action in everyday spoken English. For this reason, many of the examples sound quite natural to the reader/hearer and are easily understood.

We can identify three types of construction of words in English

57

corresponding processes of forming new words. They usually called *inflection*, *derivation* and *compounding*. While derivation and compounding are to be seen at work daily creating new words in the language, inflection simply adds the old endings to new words. The plural inflection of nouns, for example, adds /-s/, /-z/ or /-ɪz/ to singular nouns as in the everyday examples *cats*, *dogs* and *horses* and is used in a regular way by Carroll in *toves*. The main function of inflection in word-formation is, therefore, to reflect other processes, such as when a verb is derived from a noun and can, as a result, take verbal inflections: *I am hammering this nail into the wall.* Changes to the inflection system itself are rare and quite striking since they do not happen regularly in 'everyday English'. For example, English lost its second person verbal inflection (*thou goest*) over a long period of time. As a result of the stability of the inflection system, few twentieth-century poets have experimented with inflection; those who do so are known for the ungrammaticality of their work. Chapter 2 illustrated, for example, the double comparatives used by cummings in his poem *love is **more thicker** than forget*. Such experiments are rare, even in the twentieth century.

A slightly more common way of exploiting inflection for novel effect is to affix an inflection to a word in the right major word-class, but in a different minor word-class. For example, in his poem *Snow*, MacNeice uses an adjective which is not usually gradable as though it were gradable by giving it a comparative suffix: *World is **suddener** than we fancy it.* The effect is to show that just when we think we have the measure of life, it can surprise us.

The second, more common way of inventing new words is derivation, which is used frequently in colloquial language. While many nouns have derived verbs which are well established in English (e.g. *brush – to brush / mirror – to mirror*), the process is also productive for native speakers. For example, there is one group of nouns denoting tools whose corresponding verbs mean 'to use a — '. The verb *hammer* thus means 'to use a hammer' and the verb *saw* means 'to use a saw'. Children of 2–5 years will be heard uttering phrases such as 'I'm screwdrivering' or 'I'm computering', illustrating that they see this kind of derivation as a dynamic process.

The twentieth-century poets, some of whom once again are trying to return to 'the very language of men',[1] use processes of

derivation to achieve freshness in their poetry by creating new
words while appealing to the reader's familiarity with the creative
processes themselves.

The examples which could be given here are numerous, but
those which follow are chosen to illustrate the major types of
derivation and typical ways of using them in poetry. Derivation is
conveniently divided into two types; derivation using affixes and
so-called 'zero-derivation' where there is no affix and the context
alone shows that a word has changed its word-class.

If, as claimed earlier, one of the purposes or effects of derivation in poetry is to reflect the vivaciousness and inventiveness of
everyday speech, it is not surprising to find that the affixes which
are least productive outside poetry are similarly rare within it.
Prefixes, for example, are often unproductive in the modern language and any new use of such a prefix may sound rather strained.
The prefix *be-*, for example, is one which is not available to the
speaker as a productive tool and very few examples of this prefix
are to be found in modern poetry. In this line from Betjeman's
A Subaltern's Love Song: And the cream-coloured walls are **be-**
trophied *with sports*, the prefix has a flippant anachronistic effect
since the prefix sounds 'dated' in the relatively modern world of
Golf Clubs, Rovers and Austins. Auden's poem *Streams*, by
contrast, describes a *cool valley* (1.51) and *the wolds that* **begirdled**
it (1.53), attaching an outdated prefix to an outdated word. The
resulting derived word fits well into the context where Auden,
by means of a nostalgic look at events in his past, 'bemoans' the
destructive nature of human beings, while marvelling at the
capacity of nature (in particular the 'song' of running water) to
survive:

> And dearer, water, than ever your voice, as if
> Glad – though goodness knows why – to run with the
>   human race, . . .
>
>   (ll. 69–70)

There are few highly productive prefixes in modern English, but
one of the negative prefixes, *un-*, is not only common in colloquial
speech, but is used frequently in modern poetry, both in existing
and new words. Most words with the negative prefix *un-* are
adjectives:

> Meet Adam under glass in a museum
> Fleshless and most **unlovely**, . . .
>   (Francis Scarfe, *Progression*)

Some, however, are derived from verbs:

> Somewhere above the ice, **unwitnessed** storms
> Break in the darkness on the summit ridge . . .
>   (Michael Roberts, *The Secret Springs*, ll. 25–6)

The effect of using the *un-* prefix, even in an existing word, is often one of absolute passivity or neglect:

> But those who lack the peasant's conspirators,
> The tawny mountain, the **unregarded** buttress, . . .
>   (Louis MacNeice, *Poem*)

Here, MacNeice regrets the passing of the simple country life and criticises the encroaching modern, industrialised society. His use of *unregarded* emphasises the way in which modern city dwellers do not notice features of the landscape. Other uses of the prefix, however, may present the reader with an apparent contradiction as in the following line by Michael Roberts:

> of changing, and **unchanging**, sea.
>   (Michael Roberts, *The Secret Springs*, l. 20)

This line points out the fact that the sea is made up of water which constantly moves through the cycle of sea – cloud – rain – river – sea. At the same time the ocean as a whole seems not to change.

New words beginning with *un-* are quite easily understood, but are sometimes juxtaposed with established *un-* words and are consequently decoded on analogy with the established word:

> His eyes, acute and quick, are **unprotected**,
> **Unsandalled** still, his feet run down the lane, . . .
>   (Michael Roberts, *The Child*)

Here, *unsandalled* is interpreted in relation to *unprotected*, emphasising the connection between freedom and vulnerability.

One effect of using highly productive affixes is that it is not always clear when there is an established use of the affix and when it is new. It may be, for example, that both Spender and Eliot invented *unflowering* independently:

> the **unflowering** wall sprouted with guns . . .
>   (Stephen Spender, *Ultima Ratio Regum*)

> and, growing between them, indifference
> Which resembles the others as death resembles life,
> Being between two lives – **unflowering**, between
> The live and the dead nettle.
>   (T.S. Eliot, *Little Gidding* ll. 4–7)

On the other hand, Eliot may have seen the potential of Spender's word and incorporated it in his 'hedgerow' metaphor. Or, perhaps the word 'exists' anyway. In some cases it is impossible to distinguish between these conditions. Productive affixes sound so natural that English speakers find difficulty in identifying the old from the new. The poets of the twentieth century have made great use of this as other 'comfortable' examples with *un-* prefixes show:

> into the **undared** ocean
>   (W.H. Auden, *O Love, . . .*, l.43)

> Keep our Europe **undismembered**
>   (John Betjeman, *In Westminster Abbey*)

> the **unraised** hand calm,
> The apple **unbitten** in the palm.
>   (Philip Larkin, *As Bad as a Mile*)

Some poets have played on the ambiguity of the prefix *un-*. Spender, for example, writes the following lines in his poem *Fall of a City*:

> All the lessons learned, **unlearnt**;
> The young, who learned to read, now blind
> Their eyes with an archaic film . . .

Spender is commenting on the fact that the lessons of war, how-ever horrible, can be forgotten. His *unlearnt* does not have the expected meaning of 'never learnt' but like *unbutton* or *undo* in this context it is intended to convey the reversal of a process. What was learnt has been forgotten.

A frequent use of the negative *un-* prefix is as part of a negative lexical build-up within a poem. Two examples are discussed here. In Larkin's *Talking in Bed*, the poet plays with negative prefixes by apparently cancelling them. He does this in two ways: *the wind's* **incomplete unrest**.

Here Larkin creates a kind of double negative which may cause the reader to consider just how inaccurate is the popular myth that in language, as in mathematics, two negatives make a posi-tive. *Incomplete unrest* is very far from being the same as *complete rest*. A similar point is made more obviously at the end of the same poem:

> It becomes still more difficult to find
> Words at once **true** and **kind**
> Or not **untrue** and not **unkind** . . .

The poet is emphasising the fact that *true/untrue* and *kind/unkind* are not, as is popularly supposed, complementaries where the negative of one word is equal to the positive of the other. Instead he presents them as being gradable opposites (see section on oppositeness in chapter 5); there are many shades of truth and kindness in between.

Another negative build-up occurs in a poem called *1st September 1939*, written by Auden at the outbreak of war and reflecting the bleak despair which must have been felt by many observing another slide into military confrontation. The poet uses a variety of negative affixes when he speaks of: a **dis**honest decade (l. 5), the **un**mentionable odour of death (l.10), **mis**management (l. 32), help**less** governors (l. 73) and a defence**less** (l. 89) world. The poem finishes with a wish to counteract this negative build-up by expressing the wish to *Show an affirming flame*.

While there are few productive prefixes in English, productive suffixes abound and are exploited widely in modern poetry. Again poets tend to reflect colloquial usage by using most often those suffixes that are used inventively in everyday speech. However, there seems to be some restriction on this general rule since suffixes common in certain areas of modern life, such as technology and science, are notably absent from modern poetry. Examples of suffixes which are still not deemed suitable for poetic language include *-ise* and *-ation*. Exceptions to this general rule occur occasionally, but unlike the vast majority of words created by affixation, they are likely to stand out from the surrounding context. One example, from Betjeman, is used as part of a comment on the jargon used by executives:

> For vital off-the-record work – that's talking **trans
> port-wise**
> I've a scarlet Aston-Martin – and does she go? She
> flies!
> (John Betjeman, *The Executive*)

Other uses of suffixes associated with jargon may not be so humorous, but they are equally self-conscious:

> Makers' lives are spent
> Striving in their chosen
> Medium to produce a
> **De-narcissus-ized** en-
> -during excrement.
> (W.H. Auden, *The Geography of the House*)

The obvious structure of this word emphasises the self-contradictory efforts of people to appear natural and not inward-looking. Most uses of suffixes, however, tend to be less obtrusive than these examples. One particularly useful suffix, *-er*, changes a verb into an agentive noun (e.g. *baker*) or a noun describing a tool/ material into a noun describing its user (e.g. *tiler*):

> how we marked
> The lights of the **fish-spearers** and wished
> There was a moon over the cypresses, . . .

In this poem, *And Forgetful of Europe*, Geoffrey Grigson describes an idyllic scene and implicitly contrasts it with problems of war in Europe. The *fish-spearers* form part of this scene and the suffix of occupation or trade, which implies habitual or recurrent activity, makes them seem to have a static quality as though they were captured by a snapshot. A similar effect is produced in a poem by Louis MacNeice called *Autumn Journal III*:

> Most are **accepters**, born and bred to harness,
> And take things as they come, . . .

The habit of 'accepting' is here portrayed as an occupation rather than an act of will and MacNeice contrasts it with *a future of action* at the end of the poem, exhorting himself and others to:

> Cure that habit, look up and outwards
> And may my feet follow my wider glance
> First no doubt to stumble, then to walk with the
>   others
> And in the end – with time and luck – to dance.

Some suffixes create new nouns which emphasise the unity of a group of individual people or things. Larkin's ***estateful*** *of washing* in his poem, *Afternoons*, for example, establishes the housing-estate as an empty unit capable of being filled by such things as washing. In *Byzantium*, Yeats's *drunken* ***soldiery*** makes the soldiers part of the equipment of the Emperor together with his *armoury* and on analogy with other, more mundane, sets of items such as *cutlery*. Larkin also makes use of this otherwise unproductive suffix in *the old* ***tenantry*** (from *An Arundel Tomb*).

Two ways of creating adjectives by suffixation which are used readily in everyday English are also exploited widely by modern poets. The suffix *-ish* is particularly productive in the spoken language and has a colloquial effect. Three examples from Auden's poetry were given in chapter 2 in the discussion of non-standard usage: ***tigerish*** *blazer*, ***pound-noteish*** and *How* ***grahamgreenish***. These examples show up clearly the influence of the spoken style on word-formation, since they emphasise rather than underplay the 'inventedness' of the word. Another suffix *-like*, which causes a similar meaning change to *-ish*, is more common in written style and is useful to poets as an economical way of creating a simile. MacNeice, for example, uses *the* ***hive-like*** *dome* to describe *The British Museum Reading Room*, where the phrase equates the

nouns *hive* and *dome*. As well as describing the shape of the
building, connotations of *busy bees* characterise the occupants of
the library. Other examples of economical similes are found in
Spender's *flag-like faces/Of militiamen* (from *Port Bou*) and
Auden's *tigerish blazer and the **dove-like** shoe* (from *To a Writer
on His Birthday*).

The preoccupation with negation in twentieth-century poetry
is confirmed by the extensive use of the negative suffix *-less*.
Examples range from Auden's *poor in their **fireless** lodgings* (from
Spain) and Spender's ***rootless** weeds* (from *An Elementary School
Classroom in a Slum*) to Yeats's *glory of **changeless** metal* (from
Byzantium) and Eliot's ***lipless** grin* (from *Whispers of
Immortality*). As with the *-ish* and *-like* suffixes, these inventions
are so common in everyday speech that their novelty barely inter-
rupts the flow of the poem.

The final example of a derivational suffix which is used widely
in twentieth-century poetry is *-y*, which creates adjectives from
nouns. The examples of this suffix often reflect everyday spoken
usage:

> after the **droughty** downs the lanes were night
> and drowned in leaves across their **caky** ruts; . . .
> (Peter Hewitt, *Place of Birth*)

Sometimes, however, there is a reflection of other uses as in this
line from Betjeman's *A Subaltern's Love Song* which evokes the
language of advertising slogans for disinfectant:

> Into nine-o'clock Camberley, heavy with bells
> And **mushroomy**, **pine-woody**, evergreen smells.

As well as deriving new words by adding affixes to old ones,
poets have exploited another method of derivation used widely in
the language. This is often known as 'zero-derivation' since it
simply involves changing the word-class without affixes. Such
derivations can change a word from one to another of the main
word-classes: noun, adjective, adverb and verb.

Sometimes there is a musical or sound-symbolic reason why a
'zero-derived' word is appropriate as in these lines from
Ambulances by Larkin:

> For borne away in deadened air
> May go the sudden **shut** of loss . . .

Here, the word *shut* not only echoes the sounds of *sudden*, but also symbolises, by the abruptness of its final consonant, the impact of illness or death on 'ordinary' life. It is a noun created from the verb *shut* with no affixation. The reverse derivation, from noun to verb, is also common:

> The rain of London **pimples**
> The ebony street with white . . .
> (Louis MacNeice, *London Rain*)

This description of the 'spotted' effect of a road in the rain reminds the reader of nouns sharing similar meaning and a similar ending such as *speckles* and *freckles*. The sound of the verb *pimples*, therefore, is not jarring and the meaning is easily understood from the derivational process. The particular relevance of the new word in this case, however, is not sound-symbolism, but a vivid visual effect. The way that rain splashes up from a wet road is captured by the subtle difference between *spots*, *freckles* and *speckles* on the one hand and *pimples* on the other. Only the last necessarily have a raised surface. The use of a verb rather than an adjective, *pimpled*, gives the rain an active role in the proceedings.

The most frequent kind of zero-derivation found in modern poetry is the past participle form of a verb derived from a noun. For example, in *the **urned** steps* (from *To a Writer on His Birthday*), Auden changes the common sight of flower pots on steps in Mediterranean countries into something that is done to steps. The derived ·verbs usually appear as premodifiers to nouns and are therefore interpreted on analogy with well-established derived participles such as *plastered* or *decorated*.

While zero-derivation between the major word-classes is most common in both everyday English and its use in poetry, there are examples of poets creating nouns from other classes. In *Public-House Confidence*, for example, Norman Cameron uses a preposition to describe the middle management of a firm:

> The **in-betweens** and smart commission men
> Believe I must have some pull with the boss.

In *The Importance of Elsewhere*, Larkin makes another unusual zero-derivation, from adverb to noun, and imbues the word with the significance he feels it has for people living in a strange land whose *elsewhere* is their home. There is no such excuse for feeling strange, however, in your own country: *Here no **elsewhere** underwrites my existence.*

Perhaps the most subtle type of zero-derivation is to be found in work by poets such as Yeats and Eliot who change the minor word-class of a word in order to give a different emphasis. A common thread in such derivations seems to be the creation of movement verbs from static verbs. In *The Second Coming*, for example, Yeats creates a tension between the verb *slouch*, which indicates a kind of lazy posture, and the directional adverbial *towards Bethlehem* which sounds very purposeful:

> And what rough beast, its hour come round at last,
> **Slouches towards Bethlehem** to be born?

A very similar tension is set up in the following lines by Eliot from *Rhapsody on a Windy Night:*

> The street-lamp said, 'Regard that woman
> Who **hesitates toward** you in the light of the door
> Which opens on her like a grin.

The apparent contradiction here shows the ineffectiveness of hesitation when the intended direction (of movement or communication) is obvious.

Although derivation is used widely in the century's poetry, the possibilities of compounding are taken up even more enthusiastically by modern poets. A practical reason why compounds might be popular is that they are very economical. Larkin's *like a spring-woken tree* (from *Love Songs in Age*), for example, is shorter than *like a tree that has been woken by the Spring* and Laurie Lee's *salt-white house* (from *Music in a Spanish Town*) is shorter than *house as white as salt*. The last example underlines another advantage of the compound which is that it does not commit itself to a single interpretation of the relationship between the parts of the compound. Lee's example could have been alternatively paraphrased as *house that is white from the salt-spray of the sea*. Usually, however, there are clear references to established compounds as there are in the Adjective + Noun combinations which evoke patterns such as *as white as snow*: *snow white*. Some examples of this structure include Larkin's **cobble-close** *families* (from *Nothing to be said*) and Muir's *frost-grey* *hedge* (from *The Combat*).

In addition to their economy and tolerance of interpretation, compounds often contribute to the sound of a poem. Larkin's *wreath rubbish* (from *Naturally the Foundation . . .*) uses alliteration to combine the parts of the compound while the meanings of the words are stridently different in their connotations:

> That day when Queen and Minister
> And Band of Guards and all
> Still act their solemn-sinister
> **Wreath-rubbish** in Whitehall.

Compounds are constructed in many different ways in English and the creative poetic compounds reflect this diversity. Eliot's *Little Gidding* (I, ll.12–13) for example, includes a Noun + Noun combination in the following lines:

> There is no **earth smell**
> Or smell of living thing.

While Eliot could have used a more usual phrase such as *the smell of earth*, the compound enables him to imply that there is something we all recognise and will label as *earth smell* which needs no further description.

An Adjective + Noun combination from Auden's poem *To a Writer on his Birthday* illustrates the way in which compounds can contribute a useful ambiguity or economy of expression:

> **Half-boys**, we spoke of books, and praised
> The acid and austere.

Auden may be saying two different things here. First we can interpret the compound as meaning that the protagonists were each half a boy, being so close to each other they were really one person. It may also mean that they were half boy and half man, that they thought themselves grown up, but were still partly children.

Both of these interpretations are appropriate for the context where Auden makes reference to the frightening developments of history (in the 1930s) that they can no longer blissfully ignore.

In chapter 2, some compounds were mentioned that seemed to reflect the spoken language since they were the kind of compounds that speakers would invent spontaneously. These included Adjective + Adjective combinations such as Lawrence's description of the snake as *yellow-brown*. Other Adjective + Adjective combinations are not so clearly related to casual or spoken style, but can be effective in indicating a meaning for which English has no single adjective. In Philip Larkin's *Naturally the Foundation*, for example, the annual Remembrance Day ceremony at the Cenotaph in London is described as **solemn-sinister** *wreath-rubbish*. Larkin's mixed feelings about the ritual remembrance of those who died in wars, particularly of those who fought and died, are conveyed by the apparent contradiction of the two compounded adjectives. It would seem logical that either the ceremony is solemn or it is sinister; Larkin implies that its undoubted emotional effect on the spectator is the feeling we should distrust as being sinister. It is our very susceptibility to the solemnity of such an occasion that makes us vulnerable to future wars.

Other compound structures are also very common in twentieth-century poetry. Larkin's poem *Essential Beauty* draws a contrast between the world of advertisements and the real world. His advertising world is described using a number of compounds which emphasise the neatness of that idyllic world: *these* **sharply-pictured** *groves / of how life should be* (Adverb + Adjective); **Well-balanced** *families* (Adverb + Adjective); **dark raftered** *pubs* (Adjective + Adjective); **white-clothed** *ones from tennis-clubs* (Adjective + Adjective).

Other economies of expression can be gained by compounds with a participle as their second part. MacNeice, for example, in *Autumn Journal III* uses this kind of compound to dispense with the psychoanalyst as the cure for the world's troubles in 1939: *But the final cure is not in his* **past-dissecting** *fingers*. The effect of such a compound is to concentrate the force of a whole clause into a single adjective. In this case the clause would be something like 'analysts who dissect the past'. The effect of MacNeice's version lies in the visual image of an analyst as someone using their fingers on an intricate and narrowly focused dismantling operation. The useless nature of such introverted processes in the face of the world crisis in 1939 is partly conveyed by this compound.

Another highly compact compound is used in *The Second Coming* by Yeats: *The **blood-dimmed** tide is loosed*. The image of the sea water being made opaque by spilt blood is a very powerful one and enables Yeats to concentrate a number of plosive sounds, particularly alveolar plosives (/d/ and /t/) in a shorter space than if the same effect were attempted in a clause such as *the tide is made dim by blood*.

COMBINATION OF WORDS

One feature of much poetry which is particularly typical in the twentieth century is its ability to surprise the reader. A useful means of creating surprise is to juxtapose words which are not normally seen together. Traditionally this kind of juxtaposition occurred mainly as personification. In such cases an inanimate object (or abstract idea) is imbued with animate characteristics, usually by being associated with a verb or adjective which requires animacy in its object of reference. Line 398 from *The Waste Land* illustrates: *The **jungle crouched**, humped in silence*.

Here Eliot uses *the jungle* with a verb more normally associated with the jungle's inhabitants, particularly the big cats; the resulting image is one of impending danger and alert watchfulness.

Such examples would be described by linguists as 'breaking selectional restrictions'; the verb *crouched* is normally restricted to occur with animate nouns as subject and the effect of breaking this general rule is to make the subject noun, *jungle*, appear to be animate itself.

One of the poetic effects of unusual juxtaposition of all kinds is to set up a mini-metaphor by bringing together two quite different notions in order to point out their similarity. This phenomenon is illustrated by lines from *Humming Bird* by D.H. Lawrence:

> Before anything had a soul,
> While life was a heave of Matter, half inanimate,
> This little bit chipped off in brilliance
> And went whizzing through the **slow**, vast, succulent
>   **stems** . . .

Here, *stems*, which are unable to move on their own, are described as *slow*, but Lawrence is pointing out the contrast between the speed of the humming bird and the comparative inactivity of the rest of creation at a time *before anything had a soul*. After the surprise of seeing *stems* described as *slow* we quickly reach the conclusion that it is the slow growth of the plants, and possibly also their slow evolution, which is referred to here.

Universal Categories

Traditionally the most common examples of broken selectional restrictions relate to universal categories, such as animacy or concreteness. However, personification, and anthorpomorphism,[2] both used by poets throughout the ages, seem to have been diminishing in their popularity in the twentieth century, possibly as a result of more general changes in human thinking which no longer places people at the centre of the universe. There are therefore fewer appropriate opportunities for seeing the animal and inanimate worlds in human terms. Some contemporary poets, such as Ted Hughes, have deliberately set out to reverse the process and, for example, see the world as through the eyes of a hawk (*Hawk Roosting*) or muse on the instinctive nature of *Thrushes*:

> Is it their single-mind-sized skulls, or a trained
> Body, or genius, or a nestful of brats
> Gives their days this bullet and automatic
> Purpose?

Despite the move away from human-centred metaphors, there are some striking examples of broken selectional restrictions based on universal categories to be found in twentieth-century poetry. Lawrence, for example, speaks of *the sightless realm where* **darkness** *is* **awake** *upon the dark* (from *Bavarian Gentians*) where the restriction of the adjective *awake* to animate subjects is broken. Larkin describes a scene where there are **children strewn** *on steps or road* in a poem about the inevitability of death called *Ambulances*. Here Larkin breaks a restriction on the word *strewn*, which is normally used of inanimate objects and implies that there is an agent (**someone** has scattered the objects). Although the children in this scene are not dead or injured themselves, the atmosphere of general foreboding is carried over by treating them as helpless inanimates. The agent implied by the use of *strewn* can be seen as some omnipotent being who casually scatters the children over the landscape, as an artist like Lowry scatters his figures over the canvas.

As well as the reversal of features relating to animacy, word co-occurrence can challenge restrictions based on other categories such as abstract/concrete and solid/liquid. In *In the Men's Room(s)*, for example, Piercy makes the abstract noun *poem* occur first with verbs expecting a concrete, tangible object (*bore*, *cupped*) and then with a verb expecting an edible or sexual object:

> Eventually of course I learned how their eyes
>   perceived me:
> When I bore to them cupped in my hands a new
>   poem to **nibble** . . .

To be appropriate, such 'mini-metaphors' (here *poem* as *cake*, *communion bread* or *erogenous zone*) must make sense in their context. In this poem, Piercy is showing the irony of her efforts to join the male intellectual game, which result in her once again trying to please men by tempting/ feeding them intellectually/ spiritually and reaping their praise just as generations of women have fed (and are still feeding . . .) men physically.

Two examples of solids seen as liquids follow. The first comes from *The Waste Land* where Eliot's description of London, the *Unreal city*, includes the line: *A **crowd** flowed over London Bridge, so many* (l. 62). While it is not particularly unusual in English to present a crowd of people in liquid terms (people **streaming** off the buses and trains, for example), the effect in this case is of a cross-current over the path of the river. Louise Glück's description of Egyptian landscape in the poem *The Undertaking* is another variation on the well-used metaphor of fields as lakes or seas: *fields **flooded** with cotton*.

The collocation of words which clash in this way, challenging restrictions based on universal categories, has a respectable tradition in English poetry and is not noticeably more common in the poetry of the twentieth century. There is a another familiar kind of collocation which, while not universal, has a similarly general rule relating the meanings of the words brought together. There are, for example, poems where a noun relating to a part of something is made to behave like the whole,[3] by being collocated with a verb usually required to occur with the word for the whole item. For example, a body part may be used with a verb normally used of whole bodies as in *Dulce et Decorum Est* by Wilfred Owen, where the reader is challenged to look at the dead soldier and *watch the white **eyes writhing** in his face.* The verb *writhing* is normally used of limbs and torso, but the transference to the eyes of a dead soldier as they move involuntarily up to hide the pupils is one of the many powerful images in the poem.

A similar effect is gained by using one body part to replace not the whole body, but a different part. In *The Mother*, Gwendolyn Brooks captures the greedy way in which mothers who are letting their children go (i.e. grow up) still hold on to them for short periods:

> You will never leave them, controlling with luscious
>   sigh,
> Return for a snack of them, with **gobbling mother-eye**.

The idea that mothers *snack* emotionally on their growing children is the basic metaphor here, but Brooks half retracts the metaphor by juxtaposing not *mouth*, but *eye* with the eating verb, *gobbling*.

Particular Categories

Although the juxtaposition of words from different universal categories is still common, perhaps more commonly used in twentieth-century poems are collocations of contrasting words from more restricted categories. The element of surprise in such examples is greater, as can be seen from the following extract from *Evans* by R.S. Thomas:

>   It was the dark
> **Silting the veins** of that sick man
> I left stranded upon the vast
> And lonely shore of his bleak bed.

Here, the metaphor is taken from the world of geography, the old man's veins being *silted* as if they were old, slow, dried-up rivers. The process of setting up this metaphor is the same as in the last section: a word's normal context is abandoned in favour of an unusual context. In this case, the word *silt*, which is usually restricted to use with words describing rivers, streams and other water-courses, is used with a word whose referent contains a different kind of flowing liquid: blood. The difference from the previous section is that we are now dealing with words of much more restricted usage; a verb which can only have an animate subject has a lot of nouns to choose from but a verb restricted to watercourses has a smaller choice.

Notice that the more restricted a word's normal usage, the more the usual collocates of that word are conjured up by it. In the following example, from *El Sueño de la Razón*, by Jane Cooper, the usual collocates of *dislocated* are in the background, helping the interpretation of its strange collocation with *lawns*:

> Cousin, it's of you I always dream
> as I walk these **dislocated lawns** . . .

The range of words normally occurring with *dislocated* includes joints (*shoulder*, *knee*), geographical connections (*strata*) and mechanical joints. There are also common figurative uses of the word to describe the unusual perception of the world by a disturbed mind. The latter use seems particularly apt since the poem has a dedication to 'C. in a mental hospital'. The concrete uses, on the other hand contribute the idea that dislocation occurs at places of connection and the lawns can then be seen as divided from each other, by steps or possibly by flower beds. The speaker clearly feels dissatisfied by the arrangement of these lawns and the dissatisfaction echoes her thoughts about her cousin.

The unusual collocation of words is often used to bring freshness to a familiar or overused metaphor. It is almost clichéd, for example, to present *time* as something which moves and therefore has speed: *how time flies!* In *Consider*, Auden manages to capture the fleeting nature of time as well as implying a kind of escapism, by likening the *years* to migrating birds: *After some haunted* **migratory years**.

Where two words have complementary collocational ranges, it

can sometimes be effective to interchange them, as in the following example from *ofa sunday*, by Roger McGough:

> i **watch** the **newspapers** for
> hours & **browse**
> through **T.V.**

The effect of placing a static object (*newspapers*) with a verb requiring a changing or moving object (*watch*) is to emphasise the indolence of the Sunday morning and the expectation that the newspapers will actively entertain the speaker. *Browse*, on the other hand, usually requires a static object which is *looked through* but without any particular system or concentration. The television is therefore portrayed as something of this kind and the notion of channel-switching comes readily to mind.

Words with relatively small ranges of possible co-occurrence have provided the modern poet with the potential for surprise by breaking such restrictions. Even more effective, and therefore more attractive to modern poets, is the use of words whose restrictions of occurrence are arbitrarily much more limited and not based on categories at all. These are discussed in the next section.

Restricted Collocations

There is often a semantic connection between the different collocates of a word which has a restricted range of collocation. For example, the word *compound* occurs with *fracture*, *sentence*, *noun*, *interest* and these share the property described in dictionaries as 'made up of two or more parts'. However, it doesn't occur with just any word whose referent is made up of two or more parts, as can be seen from the unusual phrases, *compound shelves* and *compound reports*. The use of such a word in unusual circumstances stands out for the reader, although the process of interpretation is similar to before; the process of understanding the normal collocates is carried over to the new word, as in *Little Gidding* II by Eliot, where the narrator paradoxically recognises a 'stranger':

> The eyes of a familiar **compound ghost**
> Both intimate and unidentifiable.
>
> (ll. 42–3)

The ghost whom Eliot meets is clearly made up of a number of parts of different acquaintances from the past and the use of the adjective *compound* here gives a vivid idea of the way the parts have merged to make a whole person.

Some poets have taken the use of unusual collocations further by making them fit into the general metaphorical context of the poem. Geoffrey Hill's *Canticle for Good Friday*, for example, describes the crucifixion of Jesus in graphic terms reminiscent of a butcher's slab:

> the dulled wood
> Spat on the stones each drop
> Of deliberate blood

and

> The strange flesh untouched, carrion-sustenance . . .

In this context it is relatively unsurprising to find an adjective normally used to describe meat: ***choicest** defiance*. Its position modifying an abstract noun, *defiance*, rather than more tangible collocates such as *cuts of pork* is startling, but the meaning is clear: it is the most exquisite form of defiance to die upon the cross.

At times the normal collocations of a word serve to undermine the surface meaning of a phrase. Many of the expected nouns following the adjective *monumental*, for example, would have a negative force: *blunder, error, fiasco, farce, mistake*. There is, per-haps, something of this critical note in the phrase *monumental slithering* used in *Broadcast* by Philip Larkin to describe the music played by the string section of an orchestra whose main interest for Larkin is a woman in the audience (see chapter 8 for a full analysis of this poem).

Sometimes poets place a word in a new context to bring out its connotative value rather than its denotation. In *Fern Hill* we find the following lines:

> I lordly had the trees and leaves
> Trail with daisies and barley
> Down the rivers of the **windfall light**.

While *windfall* is most commonly used for early falling apples, and figuratively for large amounts of money, it has connotations of unexpected luck which carry over into this context describing Dylan Thomas's early life.

At the opposite end of the scale from freely occurring words (like the verb *be*) there are words which fit into the unvarying and set patterns we might class as idioms. These extreme examples of restricted collocation are usually typical of the spoken language and have therefore been little used in poetry until this century when the spoken language once again became the target of poets. Chapter 2 discussed examples from Dylan Thomas's *Fern Hill*: *once **below** a time, all the **sun** long, all the **moon** long, happy as the **heart** was long*. Another example of the creative use of a familiar expression comes from *Rough*, by Stephen Spender:

> I feared the **salt coarse** pointing of those boys
> Who copied my lisp behind me on the road.

While *salt* and *coarse* independently modify the noun *pointing*, showing the boys to be 'unrefined' (*coarse*) and 'stinging' in their comments (*salt* in a wound?), the juxtaposition of these words produces a sound sequence very similar to that of another phrase. Missing only the first unstressed syllable, it adds another dimension which is entirely appropriate in a poem dealing with bullying. The poor child had to 'run the gauntlet' each time he passed the bullies, who set up a verbal/gestural *assault course* for him.

Collocational Contradictions

The final group of examples dealing with co-occurrence of words is particularly well represented in twentieth-century poetry.[4] These examples share an apparent contradiction between the two parts of the collocation, which has to be resolved to enable an interpretation to follow. Yeats's poetry is a rich source of such tensions in the vocabulary, as the following phrase from *The Second Coming* illustrates: ***Mere anarchy** is loosed upon the world*.

More expected modifiers of *anarchy* might be *absolute* or *extreme* which show the way the state of anarchy is usually viewed by society; an extreme and threatening condition. However, Yeats does not fall into the trap of overstating his warnings as we tend to do in ordinary speech. Instead he underplays the lack of order he is predicting by the use of *mere*. The effect is to make his warning sound very grave and serious, at the same time showing that the process described is simply an inevitable downward spiral of decay rather than a positive explosion of anarchy, which would itself be a contradiction for Yeats.

A similar strategy of understating the force of a word by an unusual collocation can be seen in these lines from *Canticle for Good Friday* by Geoffrey Hill:

> (A **slight miracle** might cleanse
> His brain
> Of all attachments, claw-roots of sense) . . .

Like *anarchy*, the word *miracle* normally has an absolute meaning and is collocated with superlative adjectives such as *most amazing* or *fantastic*. In the context of Jesus' life, however, the kind of miracle being suggested by Hill is comparatively *slight*; to numb Thomas's mind so that the realisation of what was happening before his eyes would not be so painful. It also has the ring of a prayer, beseeching God to perform not the greater miracle of saving Jesus, but to provide emotional protection for Thomas.

5 Word-Choice and Meaning

WORD-CHOICE

The choice of vocabulary (sometimes called 'diction') for a poet has probably never been wider than in the twentieth century. While there has been a recurrent pattern in English poetry of writers rejecting the old-fashioned, restricted vocabulary items of their predecessors, this century has seen an unprecedented use of vocabulary from areas of life not traditionally recognised as poetic. We have already seen, in chapter 2, how the spoken language has influenced vocabulary choice in poetry, introducing more dialect words, taboo words and colloquial language than ever before. Modern poetry has also broken down barriers against scientific and technical language as Adrienne Rich demonstrates in the opening of her poem, *Waking in the Dark*:

> The thing that arrests me is
> how we are composed of **molecules** . . .

While the choice of previously unacceptable vocabulary is a feature of poetry in the twentieth century, other aspects of word-choice include subtle uses of meaning relationships which, while not new, are perhaps more frequently exploited in recent work.

MULTIPLE MEANING

> When thou hast done, thou hast not done
> For, I have more.
> (John Donne)

This excerpt from *A Hymne to God the Father* (1633), which contains a pun on the poet's name, shows that the pun is not a new feature of poetic style. Twentieth-century poets, however, have developed the pun to create a variety of subtle effects.

If we describe a pun as a play upon two (or more) meanings of a word, these meanings (often called 'senses') can be in one of four different relationships to each other. They may be homonyms which share their spelling and their sound but have no semantic connection at all: e.g. *bark* (of a tree) or *bark* (of dogs). They may be homophones which sound the same but are spelt differently: e.g. *meet* / *meat*. Or they may be homographs which are spelt the same but have different pronunciations: e.g. *minute* (60 seconds) /mɪnɪt/ or *minute* (tiny) /maɪnjuːt/. While these three relationships are accidental, the fourth, usually called polysemy, exists between related senses of a word: e.g. *wings* (of a bird) or *wings* (offstage).

Puns made on the basis of one of the three accidental relationships are likely to stand out in a text since some ingenuity may be needed to find contexts where two unrelated senses are both relevant. These highly prominent puns also tend to be humorous and are often found in jokes and advertising. Much more common in the poetry of the twentieth century are puns which play on the polysemous (related) senses of a word and which have little or no humorous effect. One example which illustrates this point comes from *The Death Bed* by Siegfried Sassoon: *Soaring and quivering in the* **wings** *of sleep*. This exploitation of the two meanings of *wings* will be discussed again later. Here it is sufficient to notice that in the context of a man's death, the effect of the word is not to make the reader smile, but rather to dwell on the abundance of meaning conjured up by the two possible readings of this line which means either 'waiting in the wings as an actor waits for the performance' or 'resting, sheltered by the wings of sleep shaped like a bird'.

Before we look at more poetic examples in detail, it is appropriate to examine the nature of polysemous meaning in English words when considered independently of their context.

Some people argue that words have no meaning in themselves and that any meaning they have is derived from their occurrence in a particular context. The fact that the word *head* immediately brings something to your mind (the top of a human body? the headteacher at your school?) probably indicates that the argument that isolated words have no meaning at all cannot be accepted. However, what is more generally accepted is that words have meaning principally by virtue of having been used in a particular way many times over. Through use, then, words acquire meaning, and in English there are words which have (so far) acquired only one meaning and words which have acquired two, three or twenty meanings. Although science and technology provide us with many words of the first sort (e.g. *cyclotron*), the words with more than one meaning tend to be commonly used words which often have their meanings added to by figurative extension. These words will usually have a central, rather obvious meaning, such as when *head* means 'top of the body', and a number of peripheral meanings which do not stand out so clearly when the word is met in isolation. The sense of *head* which means 'headteacher' is just one of a number of other meanings of this word which cluster around, and are derived from, the central meaning: the head of a river, the head on a pint of beer, a head of cattle . . . and so on. Although the central meaning of a word stands out from the others when it occurs in isolation, some contexts can make a less obvious interpretation equally appropriate. This is seen in the following line from *The Lesson* by Roger McGough, where two meanings of *head* are juxtaposed for comic effect: *The **Head** popped a **head** round the doorway.* The schoolroom context of this poem gives *headteacher* a high probability of occurrence. However, the use of the indefinite article (*a*), has the strange effect of separating the head from the headteacher's body as though he were *popping* somebody else's head round the door. This line also seems to emulate the kind of pompous and impersonal language a stereotypical headteacher would use.

Where a polysemous word is being used in more than one of its senses, but occurs only once, the resulting effect can belong to one of three groups. First, the senses may be grammatically possible in the context as well as being relevant semantically. Secondly, the senses may be grammatically possible in the context but one may be semantically prominent. Thirdly, there may be only one sense which is grammatically possible and is therefore also semantically prominent. These three groups are investigated in detail in the following paragraphs. As the discussion of examples will show, this is an over-simplified classification since there are a number of factors apart from grammar and semantics which cut across such divisions. However, it is a convenient framework for discussion and the other factors can be introduced as they arise.

The first category described above concerns words having multiple senses which are both grammatically and semantically possible in the context. One example from Stephen Spender's poem *Rough*, is the word *rough* itself: *My parents kept me from children who were **rough***. Here, this word can mean both *common, vulgar* and *physically violent*. Both of the relevant senses are adjectives and both are equally appropriate to describe the boys who form the subject of the poem. The *common* meaning is implied by the first line with the parents making their son avoid such boys. The other meaning (*violent*) is confirmed in the rest of the poem when the boys are described as having *jerking hands* and *muscles like iron*.

The next example has already been mentioned above: *Soaring and quivering in the **wings** of sleep* (*The Death Bed*: Sassoon). Both interpretations of *wings* are grammatically correct, and once identified, they seem equally appropriate in terms of meaning. But one or other of these readings may come as a surprise to the individual reader. This provides a good illustration of the active part that a reader plays in reading a literary work. Readers bring all their experience to any reading; a reader who spends time working in the theatre, for example, might identify the 'offstage' meaning of *wings* first. Further examples of such poetic 'puns' include the following: *And the weak spirit **quickens** to rebel* (from *Ash-Wednesday* by T.S. Eliot, l. 13) and *he continued with his **game*** (from *The Lesson* by Roger McGough). In the first of these examples, *quickens* could mean 'come to life' (as when babies are first felt to move in the womb), or it could mean 'to speed up'. The second example could imply a *game* such as those usually played by children, but the mention of a *shotgun* brings the sense of 'prey' or 'quarry' to mind.

Some polysemous words are used in both a semantically and a grammatically ambiguous way. The next example, from *Canticle for Good Friday* by Geoffrey Hill, uses two senses of *suffer*:

> And **suffered** to remain
> At such near distance . . .

Suffered is grammatically ambiguous since it could be either a past tense, *he suffered*, or it could represent a past participle with the auxiliary verb missing, *he (was) suffered*. The first, transitive, interpretation shows Thomas experiencing pain, the second (intransitive) states that he was allowed to remain near (by the soldiers? by Jesus?). The second, more unusual, sense may not have arisen in any other context, but it echoes Jesus' well-known phrase; *Suffer little children to come unto me* and is therefore prominent in this poem which deals with Jesus' crucifixion.

Another interesting exploitation of a polysemous word occurs in *Fern Hill* by Dylan Thomas:

> Now as I was young and easy under the apple boughs
> About the **lilting** house and happy as the grass was
>   green, . . .

The adjective *lilting* normally describes either a 'rhythmic tune' or a 'swinging movement' so that its modification of a house which neither sings nor dances indicates that it is being applied metaphorically in both its senses. Its position as a participial adjective before a noun, although semantically unusual, is grammatically acceptable (cf. *a lilting song*). This example is a long way from the type of pun found in simple jokes, since the senses are not working against each other in any way, but rather emphasise the strand of meaning which they share; a 'carefree, happy' connotation which is particularly fitting in the early, idyllic childhood context of *Fern Hill*.

Occasionally the reader comes across an unfamiliar word in a poem which could have a number of meanings, some of which may be recognised by the dictionary and some of which may be invented senses. One such example comes from *The Death Bed* by Siegfried Sassoon:

> and his mortal shore
> **Lipped** by the inward, moonless waves of death.

The word *lipped* may be new to readers, but they should be able to suggest a number of potential meanings. They may be reminded first of all of *lapped* which is very similar in form and whose meaning is appropriate in describing *waves*. *Lipped* also sounds like a form derived from the noun *lip* which could mean *touched lightly with lips* (a connection with the kiss of death) or *edged, rimmed by*. The first and second of these meanings are confirmed by the *Concise Oxford Dictionary* but the last one is not mentioned in this dictionary at least. Although interesting, it is not essential for an understanding of the poem to know which of these meanings is 'invented', which 'acknowledged' by the dictionary compilers and which intended by the poet. Like the previous example (*lilting*), this word does not so much supply a number of different readings of the line as have a 'range' of meanings which work together to create a fuller picture from a single reading. If the reader tries to imagine a visual scene of the dying man's *mortal shore* the behaviour of the *waves of death* does not seem to change significantly whichever way *lipped* is understood.

The second group of examples contains extracts where one sense of a word stands out as the main sense and the other(s) have less force, even though they are grammatically possible. The semantic context is usually responsible for emphasising one reading at the expense of the other(s) and it may lead the reader toward one of the less central senses. The following example comes from *Morning Song* by Sylvia Plath:

> The midwife slapped your footsoles, and your **bald** cry
> Took its place among the elements.

Out of context the 'hairless' sense of *bald* is more central, but its position here as modifier of the word *cry* brings the sense meaning 'stark' into relief. *Bald cry* is reminiscent of the more familiar phrase *bald statement*; it does not immediately evoke the 'hairless' sense of *bald* which is found modifying nouns like *head* and *pate*. The 'stark' sense is reinforced by the bleak surroundings of a hospital waiting room which is likened to *a draughty museum*. The 'hairless' sense is nevertheless clearly relevant to newborn babies and also finds an echo in this line.

Our reading of a polysemous word in poetry, then, is not controlled by the central meaning, although this may have some influence. One example of a word where a derived sense has become the most usual or central sense is *monumental*. Although it might literally be defined as 'pertaining to, or typical of a monument', it is now normally used to mean 'huge'. In Philip Larkin's poem,

Broadcast, the sense of 'very large in size or quantity' seems to characterise the *slithering* sounds of the orchestral strings. There is, however, also a fainter impression of its other more literal sense evoked by the setting of the concert; a large church or Town Hall. Such buildings usually contain a number of monuments and the literal meaning 'of monuments' contributes in this way to the visual image of the surroundings.

Even though a word may have various grammatically possible senses, they are not all necessarily relevant to their poetic context. There is one sense of *stagger*, for example, which is unlikely to add anything to the interpretation of the first line from *Canticle for Good Friday* by Geoffrey Hill:

> The cross **staggered** *him*.

The redundant sense of *stagger* here, is defined in the *Concise Oxford Dictionary* as 'arrange in zigzag order'. In syntactic terms this transitive sense of the verb would be expected to appear with a plural or an uncountable object such as *teabreaks* or *leave*, and it is therefore not likely to be followed by a singular pronoun as it is in this poem. It is also, of course, semantically unhelpful.

The other transitive senses of *stagger*, however, may both be implied in this line. The most obvious one, 'cause to trip or totter', clearly describes Thomas's difficulty in carrying Christ's heavy cross. For the modern reader, who largely replaces this sense of the word with a phrase such as *made him stagger*, there is a further colloquial sense which means 'astound' or 'amaze'. The awe-inspiring experience of seeing Christ crucified would make the latter sense appropriate in this context. Which of the two relevant senses is most prominent in this case probably depends on the reader's own use of the word.

The third category introduced above contains words where only one sense is possible grammatically although other senses may be semantically relevant. Geoffrey Hill's poem, *Canticle for Good Friday*, also provides an example of this type:

> carrion-sustenance
> Of **staunchest** love, choicest defiance . . .

Only the adjectival sense of *staunch* is grammatically possible here and it conveys the 'constant' and 'dependable' love of Christ. However, there is also a verb *staunch* which is revealing since it means to 'check the flow of blood' and can be applied both literally to Christ's wounds and metaphorically to the healing power of His sacrifice.

In a language like English, which has a large number of idiomatic expressions in its vocabulary, it is not surprising to find that sequences longer than one word may have multiple meanings which can be exploited in the same ways as single words. Roger McGough, for example, plays on the literal and idiomatic meanings of *teach someone a lesson* in *The Lesson*:

> I'm going to **teach you a lesson**
> one that you'll never forget.

While some phrases can be made to 'pun' just like single words, the freedom to place words together also provides for new types of ambiguity. One possibility is to juxtapose words so that they echo a well-known phrase. One such example from *Rough* by Stephen Spender was discussed in chapter 4:

> I feared the **salt coarse** pointing of those boys
> Who copied my lisp behind me on the road . . .

Superficially, *salt* and *coarse* form a short sequence of adjectives, each independently modifying the noun *pointing*. However, the phrase *assault course* is also evoked by these two words since *salt* is almost a homophone of *assault* and *coarse*, *course* are homophones.

A final example in this section will show that there are still further ambiguities that can be created, not by grammatical or semantic ambiguity in the words themselves, but by the reference that the words have in the poem. The example comes from *A Hairline Fracture* by Amy Clampitt:

> the **pneumatic haste** of missed
> trains, the closing barrier – . . .

On a first reading, *pneumatic haste* seems to describe the pneumatically controlled doors of a London Underground train which leaves the station just as the couple who feature in the poem arrive on the platform. The train might therefore be personified and seen as being in a hurry. However, since the word *haste* is more normally used to describe people in a hurry, this inter- pretation gives *pneumatic* a new emphasis as the hurrying couple are both suffering from hay fever. They are probably wheezing from the combined effects of this affliction and of running to catch the train.

SIMILARITY OF MEANING

In this section we shall consider the poetic use of different word- forms which are semantically connected. The previous section explored the potential grammatical and semantic differences between polysemous senses of a single word-form. Very often these different senses of a word can be allocated to different 'lexical fields': groups of words whose members share the most general part of their meaning. *Assemble*, for example, has two senses (at least) which belong to separate lexical fields:

assemble (a)	assemble (b)
gather	build
collect	construct
come together	put together
congregate	

These senses of *assemble* also have different grammatical features; *assemble* (a) can occur with or without an object while *assemble* (b) (when used in the active voice) must be followed by an object. You can say *She assembled the students. The students assembled* (a) or *She assembled the model kit*, but not *The model assembled* (b).

Groups of partial synonyms (or lexical fields) such as those shown above are a widespread feature of English. The term 'synonym' is popularly understood as indicating that words mean exactly the same but such synonyms occur very rarely, even in English which is renowned for its lexical redundancy. However, the significant property of lexical fields is that their members share their most important aspects of meaning.

If every word-sense can be divided into a number of semantic 'features', the members of a lexical field will all share the features which, for example, are most likely to occur first in a dictionary definition. So verbs which describe walking in English may all share semantic features which describe them as movement verbs and specify that the subject would normally be an animate being with legs. They may then differ in their more specific semantic features, grammar, connotations, collocations or derived forms. For example, there are differences of connotation between *perambulate* (formal) and *walk* (colloquial) and differences of more particular semantic features between *stroll* (in a leisurely manner) and *march* (in a military manner).

Water by Philip Larkin is one poem which is constructed around lexical fields. The poem suggests *water* as a suitable symbol for religious worship and the two lexical fields which form the basis of Larkin's vocabulary in the poem are *water* and *religion*. The *water* field includes the word *water* itself, *fording*, *sousing* and *drench*. Note that *souse* and *drench* are quite close in meaning, although they differ in their collocations. *Souse* is a cooking term and would usually be used to describe some kind of food which is being pickled (a herring, for instance). *Drench*, on the other hand, is often applied to people and their clothes when rain, sea or some other source of wetness has soaked them. In this context, though, the similarity of meaning seems to be important; Larkin wants to emphasise the abundance of water in his religion and this is something that both *souse* and *drench* convey. It is also worth considering why, for example, he chose *souse* instead of *soak*, which has a less specialised meaning. It could be that he intended the association with drunkenness (*pickled*) that some readers may pick up. Or he may have chosen *souse* for its longer vowel and fricative ending symbolising a drawn-out process more effectively than the sounds of the word *soak*.

The *religious* field introduced by Larkin contains a number of words whose central or only meaning is religious: *religion*, *church*, *liturgy* and *devout*. There are also some words which have associations with religious rites or symbolism: *east*, *raise*, *light*, *congregate*, *images* and *endlessly*. The latter group are interesting because none of them has any necessary connection with religious vocabulary out of context but they are drawn into this lexical field by the religious context. *Congregate* is normally synonymous with *assemble* (sense (a) above), but here it brings to mind a derived noun, *congregation*, which instead of meaning simply 'a group of people gathered together', usually has a more specialised meaning

WORD-CHOICE AND MEANING 89

which adds 'in a church or other religious place of worship' to this definition. *Endlessly* is also interesting, because it evokes a similar word with strong religious connotations: *eternally*. Whereas the use of the conventionally religious term would have raised no questions, the use of a 'near-synonym' such as *endlessly* causes the reader to think about the meaning of these terms and the differences between them. *Endlessly*, for example, is often used to describe insistent and boring events such as telephone conversations or lectures. This word adds a new dimension to the poem, bringing the high religious tone down to a more mundane level with Larkin perhaps implicitly imposing on the followers of 'his' religion the same boredom that he has suffered in church services.

The two lexical fields exploited in this poem are also interrelated. Although Larkin seems to be suggesting that he has thought of a new religious symbol, water already has many connections with the Christian religion. This irony, that his 'new' idea is not in fact new, underlies the whole poem. Like the honorary members of the religious field discussed above, the 'water' words also suggest religious practices and stories. *Fording* reminds us of Baptism in rivers and Jesus walking on the water. *Sousing* and *drench* also remind us of baptism by immersion. Despite their evocative power, these words would not normally be used to describe the practices they bring to mind here whereas even the peripheral members of the religious field such as *light* or *raise* might be found in conventional religious descriptions.

Although some poems have such interrelated fields of words as their most prominent linguistic feature, many modern poems exploit fields of related words as just one of a range of linguistic effects. One such poem is *A Hairline Fracture* by Amy Clampitt (described in detail in chapter 8) where the most striking field of words introduced is taken from geology. The geological metaphor is set up in the first two stanzas with the use of *eroding* and *upper reaches*. But a more closely connected set of words describing geological faults and all used metaphorically to describe the breakdown of a relationship are concentrated in the final verse:

> it was as though we watched the **hairline fracture**
> of the quotidian widen to a **geomorphic fissure**,
> its **canyon edge** bridged by the rainbows of a terror . . .

As with Larkin's use of *endlessly* rather than *eternally*, here the poet avoids the usual clichéd phrasing but presents a similar idea in new words. She rejects one member of this geological field which has been taken into normal usage to represent the distance between human beings – *gulf* – but uses other members of the same field for the purpose. Common use of one member of a lexical field in a particular metaphorical way enables the poet to transfer other members of the same field to a similar metaphorical use with no problems of understanding, the process already being familiar to English speakers. By avoiding *gulf* itself, Clampitt also achieves a freshness which may cause the reader to reflect on the metaphorical process.

This lexical field also illustrates a technique of using related words in a progressive sequence. The rather slow disintegration of *erosion* increases in speed and effect through *fracture* which implies a split but with no separation of the two halves, and *fissure* where the parts are separated, but not very far, and where the division runs deep to *canyon* where the division is both deep and wide. Any lexical set whose members are related by the extent or intensity of a single semantic feature could be exploited in this way.

Leaving behind the uses of lexical fields which emphasise both the similarity in meaning between the words and the differences, we can see that in other uses of lexical fields the similarities are prominent. The occurrence of *closed*, *fastened* and *shut* in *Ambulances* by Philip Larkin seems primarily to focus on the finality of death and the absolute separation from the world that comes with illness. The effect of using partial synonyms like these is to intensify the meaning that they share. This is similar to a technique used in normal conversation when the feature being described is so 'xx' that a number of different words are needed to express it; 'It's wonderful . . . fantastic . . . brilliant!'

A similar effect is achieved in the same poem with *momently*, *for a second* and *sudden* which together reinforce the common part of their meaning to describe the impact of unexpected illness.

The existence of works such as Roget's *Thesaurus* shows that the relationship between words forming lexical fields in English is recognised independently of context. In context, however, the poet has the opportunity to create new lexical fields, using words which do not necessarily share the most central of their semantic features, but share some feature which is brought into prominence by their juxtaposition. The poem *Morning Song* by Sylvia Plath has a group of words which are mostly listed in separate groups by Roget: *echo, magnify, mirror, reflect.*

Although these words have considerable differences of meaning, in the poem they all change the perceptions of the newborn infant in some way, either aurally or visually, and therefore take on a coherence they do not share outside this context. Another example of a created field of words occurs in *The Death Bed* by Siegfried Sassoon: *floating, soaring, sliding, drifting.* These words would also belong to different groups of partial synonyms in a thesaurus but here their shared feature of 'smooth movement' comes to the forefront.

OPPOSITE MEANINGS

As speakers of English, we are all aware that some words in the language have 'opposites'. We are taught to recognise such distinctions at an early age and because many of the oppositions are important in our everyday lives, we tend to regard them as absolutes. However, there is no linguistic reason why these pairs of words should be considered special. Conventional opposites in English are referred to as 'antonyms' and from this name it might be assumed that they were the exact opposite of 'synonyms'. Whereas synonyms coincide roughly in meaning, antonyms might therefore be seen as differing completely in meaning. This would not be a very useful relationship to describe and it would be difficult to decide whether the words concerned were entirely different. For example, how much meaning do the words *cabbage* and *equality* share? Or *horoscope* and *felt tip pen*? In fact, antonyms are simply a special kind of partial synonym which share much of their meaning but differ radically in one prominent semantic feature. *Black* and *white* share a concern for colour, but whereas *black* is an absence of all colours, *white* occurs when all colours of the visible spectrum are present at the same time. *Push* and *pull* both refer to intentional movement of an object but in a direction which is *away from the mover* or *toward the mover* respectively. The conventional nature of oppositeness is revealed when a near-synonym is substituted for each of a pair of accepted opposites. It is immediately clear, for example, that *shove–yank* are not opposites in the popular sense, though they seem to differ from each other in the same (directional) way as *push–pull*.

A number of different types of oppositeness are represented in modern poetry. 'Gradable' antonyms such as *hot–cold* and *big–small* allow for comparative forms such as *hotter*, *colder* as well as intermediate expressions such as *cool* and *warm*. This kind of opposition forms the basis of one cummings poem already mentioned in chapters 2 and 4 which begins;

> love is **more thicker** than forget
> **more thinner** than recall . . .

'Converses' differ from gradable antonyms in the following way; at the same time as one of the converses describes one person (or thing), the other must describe another person (or thing). While someone is *buying*, there must be someone else *selling*. If one person can be described as a *wife*, there must be someone else who is her *husband*. An example of converses can be seen in the following line from T.S. Eliot's poem *Ash-Wednesday*: *Wavering between the **profit** and the **loss***. Although *profit* and *loss* are both used to show the swing in fortunes of the poet, their converse relationship reminds us that there is necessarily always someone at the other extreme of fortune.

'Complementaries' (*dead/alive* or *female/male* for example) are pairs of words which have a special logical relationship. If one of the words is true, it denies the other, and vice versa. If I am *alive*, I cannot also be *dead*; if you are *male*, you are not *female*. Another poem by cummings uses this kind of logical relationship to create new complementaries: *for whenever men are **right** they are not **young***. This line creates a complementary relationship between *right* and *young* by saying that if one is true the other cannot be true. By setting a conventional pair of complementaries (*right/wrong*) against a pair of gradable antonyms (*old/young*), cummings ignores the middle ground between young and old in a manner which reflects the youthful enthusiasm of this poem. The poem suggests the equations *young* = *wrong* and *old* = *right* and implies that there is nothing in between.

In addition to the different types of opposition illustrated above, there are a number of ways in which any pair of opposites can be exploited in poetry. In *Wintering* Sylvia Plath uses a number of conventional oppositions that reinforce each other's meaning. The dark cellar is described as *black* as are the bees when they mass together in the cold weather. These words are set against the *light* of the torch in the cellar, the *white* of the refined syrup which replaces the bees' winter store of honey and the *warm days* which carry a hint of spring.

Another use of opposition in poetry is based on the readers' familiarity with conventional oppositions and the use of a slightly unusual word to replace one of the opposites: *Shining, it was* **Adam** *and* **maiden**. This use of *maiden* instead of *Eve* in *Fern Hill* has the effect of enhancing the music of the phrase by echoing the /m/ and /d/ sounds of *Adam*. But it may also have several other effects. For some readers it may serve to dissociate the 'first woman' from the evil with which Christianity has associated the name *Eve*. For others it may make the identity of the first woman seem less important than that of the first man, *Adam*. The 'pure' and 'innocent' connotations of the replacement word, *maiden*, are also absent from the usual understanding of *Eve*. Indeed, Eve is often perceived as the original 'hussy' as a result of her tempting of Adam. Whatever the effects, intended or not, the phrase cannot be passed over as could the more familiar *Adam and Eve*.

As well as changing the form of one of the members of an opposite pair, the familiar notion can be challenged by a change in their order of occurrence. Many opposites typically occur in a fixed order; e.g. *black and white*. Some pairs, such as *birth and death*, occur in an order which is logically based; birth precedes death. In the poem *Ash-Wednesday* (extract: Allot, 1982), T.S. Eliot uses this opposition to encapsulate life in one line: *The dreamcrossed twilight between* **birth** *and* **dying**. He later reverses their order to describe the spiritual experience of death and rebirth which is an important Christian symbol: *This is the time of tension between* **dying** *and* **birth**. In both examples, Eliot also changes the usual form of *death* to *dying*. In the first, physical, context this has the effect of emphasising the relatively long process of physical death which is often said to begin at birth. In the spiritual interpretation the use of the participial form *dying* may convey the repetitive and continuous nature of sacrifice and self-denial in the Christian life.

A common feature of polysemous words is that their different senses may have different opposites. By unexpectedly using the opposite of a different sense of the word, the poet can make the reader revise their understanding of a previous line: *death (having lost*) *put on his universe.* In this poem by cummings, the use of *lost* with no following object leads the reader to understand it as meaning the opposite of won. This interpretation is reinforced by the gambling scene which unfolds in the following lines. The first line of the second stanza, however, presents us with the opposite of another sense of *lose*: *Love (having found) wound up such pretty toys.* This causes the reader to question whether death had not lost a game in the first line, but had mislaid something.

Apparent contradictions are often constructed in twentieth-century poetry by juxtaposing opposites: *Teach us* **to care** *and* **not to care**. In this example from *Ash-Wednesday,* Eliot uses negation to create the contradictory effect which is resolved by the poly-semy of the word *care.* This line can be read as meaning that we should have a conscience for the world (*care* a) but not worry too much about ourselves (*care* b).

Other contradictions are not so readily explained. They are often used to try and capture the conflicting feelings that people have about certain fundamental aspects of the world such as space and time. Our everyday conversations are sprinkled with these paradoxes expressing, for example, the feeling that you have been in a place for a long time alongside the feeling that you have only just arrived.

As with time, people often have ambivalent perceptions of space, and distance in particular. The first example of such contra-dictions of distance comes from *Canticle for Good Friday* by Geoffrey Hill:

> And suffered to remain
> At such **near distance** . . .

Thomas is feeling the pain of being so near to Jesus on the cross, but separated from him by a huge gulf of experience. This feeling of being physically close to, but emotionally or spiritually distant from someone is familiar to the reader and hardly even presents itself as a contradiction. The second example, from *A Hairline Fracture* by Amy Clampitt, describes the experience of seeing something 'up close' (in this case London) that has always been thought of as distant:

> by the miraculous rift in the look of things
> when you've just arrived – **the remote up close** . . .

Finally, many poets use the relationship of oppositeness to set words which have no conventional opposite against each other. Philip Larkin, for example, based one of his early love poems on the conflict between what he saw as the essentially transitory nature of love and the lover's fervent hope that 'this time' it would last for ever. The poem begins by setting up a pair of accepted opposites:

> Is it for **now** or for **always**,
> The world hangs on a stalk?

By using a parallel construction in the next two lines, Larkin implies that the words which replace *now* and *always* are also opposites:

> Is it a **trick** or a **trysting-place**
> The woods we have found to walk?

The next stanza continues to set up new oppositions, *mirage/miracle* and *sham/sign*, by using similar parallel constructions. These oppositions are linked by the similarity of meaning between *trick*, *mirage*, *sham* on the one hand and *miracle*, *sign* on the other. The final stanza, however, challenges the original opposition, and thereby also the created oppositions. The challenge is based on a philosophical argument that *always* is simply made up of a series of *nows* and the two notions are therefore compatible rather than contradictory:[1]

> I take you for now and for always,
> For always is always now.

6 Grammatical Structure

We have already noticed that poetry in the twentieth century has been freed from rigid constraints on poetic structure. This has meant that poets had to compensate for the loss of traditional poetic form by using the resources of the language to the full. One result is that grammatical structure has been exploited more extensively than in previous eras. This chapter illustrates the main uses of grammatical structure in poetry, including the exploitation of phrase structure and clause structure, the echoing of spoken style, the use of parallel structures and repetitions, tense, word order and finally the symbolic use of grammatical elements.

PHRASE STRUCTURE

Noun Phrases

The noun phrase is a very versatile tool in English, since it may consist of a simple noun as in *I like coffee*, but more frequently has a number of premodifiers as in the phrase ***this strong hot*** *coffee* and/or some postmodifiers which may be prepositional phrases as in *the coffee **on the table*** or subordinate clauses as in *the coffee **that the children knocked over***.

Poets have always been aware of the potential in noun phrases, and those of the twentieth century are no exception. There are many examples of quite simple noun phrases used, often in quick succession, to conjure up a vivid scene in the reader's imagination. A good example comes from Craig Raine's poem *The Grocer*, where two lines contain four noun phrases all of which have simple premodification and head noun only:

The grocer's hair is parted like **a feather**
by **two swift brushes** and **a dab of brilliantine** . . .

Many simple noun phrases in twentieth-century poetry are the vehicles for the kind of semantic effects discussed in chapter 4. Douglas Dunn's poem *Modern Love*, for example, includes the line *Enjoying minutes of a* **rented silence**, where the collocation of *rented* with *silence* gives the reader pause to consider how we normally think of rents as being paid for tangible material goods, not for abstract 'freedoms' like the right to some peace and quiet. A structurally simple noun phrase, then, can be the beginning of a complex train of thought which, in this case, traces the connection between the modern world and money.

While simple noun phrases may carry other effects, there is abundant use of the more complex noun phrase to surprise or gratify the reader/hearer. There may be, for example, a surprising number of premodifiers before the head noun is reached, as in this line from *Exposure* by Wilfred Owen: *Our brains ache, in the* ***merciless iced east*** *winds that knive us*. . . . Here, the three adjectival premodifiers emphasise the cutting edge of the wind partly by their sounds which include the /s/ phoneme four times, followed twice by the sharp sound of a voiceless plosive /t/ in the words /aist/ (iced) and /iːst/ (east).

Although we use multiple premodifiers in everyday English, they tend to be rather predictable in their combinations. The noun *pebble*, for example, might normally be preceded by the adjectives *smooth* and *round*. Similarly, the noun *idea* might be prefaced by positive adjectives such as *brilliant* and *new* or by negative ones such as *terrible* and *clichéd*. Poets, however, make use of surprising combinations such as the description, in Stephen Spender's poem *The Pylons*, of *crumbling roads/ That turned on* **sudden hidden villages**. Although we might not be surprised to find the adjective *hidden* describing villages, the adjective *sudden* is more commonly used to describe occurrences and ideas. The two adjectives together, although apparently contradictory, show that the villages are *hidden* until the last moment, when they are *suddenly* noticed. Their combination is especially gratifying because they share so much of their sound: /sʌdn/, /hɪdn/.

If poets use the premodifiers in noun phrases, they have even more scope with postmodifiers, which can form an indefinitely long list as in these lines from *The Harvest Bow* by Seamus Heaney:

> In wheat **that does not rust**
> **But brightens as it tightens twist by twist**
> **Into a knowable corona**,
> **A throwaway love-knot of straw**.

Relative clauses (often beginning with *that* or *which*) are one way of spinning out the noun phrase until the reader almost loses the thread of the clause. Of course, in the case of Heaney's poem, the description of the plaiting and weaving of a corn doll is suitably matched by the intricate structure of the phrases.

As with the repetition of simple, premodified noun phrases, a build-up of noun phrases that are postmodified in the same way as each other can also be effective. In *Woman Enough* Erica Jong, for example, uses a list of noun phrases to illustrate the kind of life her grandmother had lived:

> Because my grandmother's hours
> were apple cakes baking,
> & dust motes gathering,
> & linens yellowing
> & seams and hems
> inevitably unravelling – . . .

The use of present participles (*-ing* forms) to postmodify the head nouns gives an idea of the endlessness of the grandmother's various tasks. The repetition of the structure emphasises the need for simultaneous action on all fronts to keep the household in order.

Verb Phrases

The verb phrase is pivotal in English sentences and although it may be omitted altogether in minor sentences (as we saw in chapter 2) it has fewer options for creative variation than the noun phrase because of its rather rigid structure. The verb phrase, then, may consist of a main verb alone, as in the clause *Freda sang*. There may, however, be up to four auxiliary verbs preceding the main verb including the passive auxiliary *be* as in *She **was arrested***, the progressive auxiliary *be* as in *She **was shouting***, the perfective auxiliary *have* as in *She **has protested*** and one of the modal verbs such as *might* as in *She **might succeed***. Although verb phrases containing four auxiliaries before the main verb can occur, they are rare: *I **might have been being beaten***. More common are combinations of two auxiliaries followed by a main verb: *They **will have eaten**, I'm sure*; *We **have been swimming** in the river.*

The importance of verb phrases in English clauses and their rigid structure mean that they are the least affected of all clause elements by the experiments of even the most linguistically daring poets. The poetry of e.e. cummings is renowned for its linguistic inventiveness, but as the opening line of one of his untitled poems shows, the verb phrase is left intact: *Anyone **lived** in a pretty how town.*

The range of uses of different verb phrase structures are as wide in twentieth-century poetry as they are in everyday English usage. The most detailed example given here is the use of the simple present tense, but other verb forms could also illustrate the point. As well as indicating an activity or event occurring in present time (*I **dance***), the present tense can be used to give vibrancy to a story set in the past, indicate a habitual or repetitive action, or show a 'natural' tendency. The first of these uses can be seen in R.S. Thomas's poem *Tramp* which opens with the clause *A knock at the door/ And he **stands** there*. The arrival of the tramp is seen all the more vividly because the verb is in the present tense. Habitual or repetitive action is implied by the verbs in the following lines from *Green Ice* by Vivien Finch: *you **give** me your throat to taste; you **forbid** me to regret*. Finally, the present tense is used by cummings to indicate a kind of 'natural' force which swings like a pendulum between the extremes of knowledge and ignorance:

> all ignorance **toboggans** into know
> and trudges up to ignorance again . . .

The present tense in this example is used as if it were representing a given, universal law and in this way cummings makes a strong claim for his observations.

Other verb forms are also used in straightforward ways. The past tense may be used for storytelling as in *Snake* by D.H.

Lawrence, which opens with the line: *A snake came to my water-trough*. The progressive form may indicate continuing action, as in *For my sister* by Louise Glück: *Far away my sister is moving in her crib*. The modal verbs *will/shall* are often used with a main verb to indicate future time, especially in the kind of poetry declaring love and making promises. An example comes from *Don't Worry/ Everything's Going to be All Right* by Adrian Henri: *And every poem I write will have your name in it*. Finally, the relatively unexceptional use of verb phrases can also be illustrated by a sequence of verb phrases in Yeats's *Sailing to Byzantium* which uses a wide range of forms: *That is no country . . .* (present); *unless/ Soul clap its hands . . .* (subjunctive); *I have sailed the seas . . .* (perfective); *I shall never take my bodily form . . .* (modal).

One form of verb phrase which has a particular stylistic impact is the modal verb *may* used with the first person pronoun to make a request: *may I be mown down at dawn/ by a bright red sports car. . . .* This example from Roger McGough's poem *Let Me Die a Youngman's Death* is typical of a secular questioning of 'fate' or 'life' or some other authority in the absence of poetry's traditional authority which was God (or gods in the Greek and Roman traditions). Rarely in the twentieth century is God addressed openly. The reader may conclude that Louis MacNeice is addressing a deity when he finishes one section of his *Autumn Journal* with the same verbal form, *may I . . .*, but a more likely interpretation in the face of the despair and brutality of war is that MacNeice is simply expressing a cherished hope for his own (and others') future:

> may I cure that habit, look up and outwards
> And may my feet follow my wider glance
> First no doubt to stumble, then to walk with the
>   others
> And in the end – with time and luck – to dance.

CLAUSE STRUCTURE

It should be noted at this point, that the sentences used in the poetry of the twentieth century vary from the most simple declarative clause, such as the opening of Mary Dorcey's poem *First Love*: *You were tall and beautiful* to very long sentences with many embedded clauses and phrases such as the final section of

Wilfred Owen's *Dulce et Decorum Est*. Simple clauses are perhaps more common in the poetry of the late twentieth century than in earlier times. The recurrent call by poets for simple, accessible language has resulted in syntactic simplicity as well as the more frequent introduction of colloquial, everyday vocabulary. Sylvia Plath's poetry often achieves elegance through syntactic simplicity as in her poem *Poppies in July* which contains the Subject + Verb sentence describing the poppies: *You flicker*. Similarly, Jennifer Armitage's poem *To Our Daughter* includes the sentence *She is our child* which consists of a single clause containing Subject, Verb and Complement. There are also numerous examples of SVO (Subject + Verb + Object) clauses as in this sentence from *The Dream* by Auden: *Our whisper woke no clocks*. Here, the effect is partly gained by the collocation of an inanimate object, *clocks*, with a verb requiring animate objects, *woke*. The night seemed endless to the lovers, unbroken even by the sound of clocks. The simplicity of the structure in such an example enables the effect of the collocation to be fully appreciated. Simplicity of outlook is also the hallmark of many of Ted Hughes's animal and bird subjects. The hawk in *Hawk Roosting* is very clear about its aims and pleasures in life; the SVA (Subject + Verb + Adverbial) clause opening the poem emphasises the hawk's self-assured nature: *I sit in the top of the wood*.

Although simple clause structures are to be found in increasing quantities through the twentieth century, in syntax, as in other linguistic areas, poets use the full range of possibilities. There are, for example, innumerable subordinate clauses to be found, many of them functioning as adverbials of time, place, manner or cause. In Josephine Miles's poem *Summer*, for example, the opening two lines consist of an adverbial clause giving a setting for the main clause in both space and time:

> When I came to show you my summer cottage
> By the resounding sea,
> We found a housing project building around it . . .

Other adverbial clauses set the scene in terms of the causal relationship between subordinate and main clause. Auden's poem *The Dream* begins with a complex sentence contradicting the usual connection between the night and dreams:

Dear, **though the night is gone**,
Its dream still haunts today . . .

These uses of subordination reflect normal everyday English
usage in a straightforward way. More typical of descriptive and
imaginative prose and poetry are examples of long adverbial
clauses after the main clause of a sentence, as in the following
lines from *Knowing* by Mary Coghill:

I dug in with all the spirit of spring
delightfully teased by the sweet scent
of the freshly turned soil . . .

Such clauses, containing a non-finite verb form (an *-ed* form, an *-ing*
form or an infinitive), are frequently found in twentieth-century
poetry as in other eras. The main innovation of this century is the
occurrence of such clauses in the absence of a main clause, thus
forming one kind of minor sentence. Chapter 2, on spoken language,
dealt with minor sentences in detail since they partly reflect a modern
poetic concern with the colloquial. However, there are some
examples of such 'unattached' subordinate clauses which are more
descriptive than colloquial as a result of having no absolute time reference in the form of a finite verb. For example, *Woman Skating* by
Margaret Atwood opens with a description of a wintry scene which
turns out to be a memory flashback. The static nature of such cameos
in the mind's eye is emphasised by the lack of finite verb phrases; all
the verbs in the opening three stanzas are participles. The first three
lines, forming one minor sentence, illustrate this point:

A lake **sunken** among
cedar and black spruce hills;
late afternoon.

The effect is that of stage directions, setting the scene, but allowing for only an anticipation of any action.

PARALLEL STRUCTURES

There has been widespread use of parallel structure in twentieth-
century poetry and this has partly offset the loss of rigid poetic

form mentioned earlier. Sometimes repetitions of structurally simple elements result in lists and these have been used at times for poetic effect. The first example of this technique is a short sequence of noun phrases from *Thrushes* by Ted Hughes:

> those delicate legs
> Triggered to stirrings beyond sense – with **a start,**
> **a bounce, a stab** . . .

The short phrases containing single-syllable words are symbolic of the short, sharp movements of the thrushes as they dive to catch a worm or an insect . A more complex example of the use of lists is the whole of the poem *You're* by Sylvia Plath, where the title contains the subject (*you*) and the main verb (*are*) and the rest of the poem consists of a list of complements to the title's structure. The opening lines give an idea of the variety of complements assigned to the unborn baby, subject of the poem:

> *You're*
> Clownlike, happiest on your hands,
> Feet to the stars, and moon-skulled . . .

There are a number of other ways in which poets have used repetition to give structure, and sometimes add music, to their poetry. They occasionally repeat exactly the same words, in the same order, as in Sylvia Plath's poem *Mushrooms*: *So many of us! / So many of us!* The repetition in this case emphasises the huge number of mushrooms and adds to the sense of surprise. T.S. Eliot also opens his poem *VI* from the *Ash-Wednesday* sequence with a series of repetitions:

> Although I do not hope to turn again
> Although I do not hope
> Although I do not hope to turn . . .

The slight variations here emphasise the different meaning of the word *hope* in line 2 when it is used without an object, implying a general hopelessness. The repetition itself sets up a rhythm which remains in the background for the rest of the poem. It is as though these lines set the breathing pattern of the speaker while the following lines give a commentary on the speaker's life, which is described as *The dreamcrossed twilight between birth and dying*.

More common than exact repetition is the use of a repeated structural framework, realised with different words each time as in this excerpt from *Snake* by D.H. Lawrence:

> Was it cowardice, that I dared not kill him?
> Was it perversity, that I longed to talk to him?
> Was it humility, to feel so honoured?
> I felt so honoured.
>
>   (ll. 31–4)

As well as replacing some of the rhythm that was lost in the change from traditional forms to free verse, this repetition of structure clearly illustrates the speaker's confusion about his reactions to the snake. It sets into relief the nouns *cowardice, perversity* and *humility* and causes the reader, as well as the speaker, to consider the mixed emotions aroused by the presence of the snake at his water trough.

Another example of repeated structures filled with different words, taken from *The Death Bed* by Siegfried Sassoon, has been explored in chapter 3 in connection with the onomatopoeic words:

> He **swallowed**, unresisting; **moaned** and **dropped**
> Through crimson gloom to darkness; . . .

The conjunction of three simple past tense verbs shows the wounded soldier's progression from consciousness to a kind of semi-conscious state. A similar triad is used later in the same stanza: *He **dipped** contented oars, and **sighed**, and **slept***. This second progression moves him from the restlessness of the semi-conscious state toward a more peaceful sleep. Again, there are three stages, but they differ from the first sequence. The use of the conjunction 'and' twice in the second extract gives a feeling of smooth transition rather than the stilted and unconnected swallowing and moaning of the first extract. It is also worth noting that the first extract continues onto the next line with an adverbial describing the passage of his mind towards oblivion. The second extract, however, stops more decidedly with a full stop after 'slept', giving the reader the impression that the soldier is now sleeping undisturbed by dreams or nightmares.

The use of parallel structures, therefore, can be seen as contributing to the music of a poem but can also be used to point out similarities or highlight differences between different sections of a poem.

TENSE AND TIME

As the heading of this section implies, time and tense are not in a simple relationship in English. The same verbal form may be used to signify a number of different time relationships in different contexts. A concern with time is reflected in the poetry of the century, with all possible means of exploiting the verbal and adverbial system of the language being used. Some of the examples in this section could just as easily have been treated in the section on the verb phrase or in the section on parallel structures. However, there is a separate point to be made about the creative use of time and tense which justifies a separate section.

A relatively simple example of the use of tense is the poem *Welsh Landscape* by R.S. Thomas which conjures up the atmosphere of the past, while using present tense verbs. Two lines illustrate the theme and form:

> You **can**not live in the present,
> At least not in Wales.

The tension between the tense of the verbs and the 'past' which is constantly evoked is symbolic of the tension in the poem between people who live there (in the present) and the oppressive past which (Thomas suggests) they cannot escape. Apparent contradictions of time can also be created by juxtaposing a verb in one tense with an adverb suggesting a different tense. The opening line of *Fern Hill* (Dylan Thomas), for example, achieves a childlike emphasis on the *here and now*, while describing events in the past: ***Now** as I **was** young and easy under the apple boughs*. A more subtle use of time is to be found in *Childhood is the Kingdom Where Nobody Dies* by Edna St Vincent Millay. Much of the poem uses the present tense with a habitual meaning as in the following extract:

> Distant relatives of course
> **Die**, whom one never has seen or has seen for an
>   hour, . . .

But just as the reader gets used to the apparent generalisations, some particular events are recalled to illustrate the general point, and the fact that they are real is revealed by the abrupt switch to past tense verbs. The following lines follow the previous quotation:

> And they **gave** one candy in a pink-and-green striped
>   bag, or a jack-knife,
> And **went** away . . .

The effect of this failed attempt to generalise, resulting in a specific anecdote about the child's disillusionment with adults, is a childlike self-centredness which is appropriate in the poem. It ends with three short lines containing present tense verbs no longer used for habitual action but referring to present time, clearly bringing the narrative up to date. The whole poem then seems like a retrospective meditation by an adult on different attitudes to death experienced at different ages. The pretence of generalising, to protect the narrator from exposing her feelings, is achieved in this final part of the poem not by tense, but by the use of the impersonal second person pronoun, *you*, which the reader interprets as meaning *I*:

> Your tea **is** cold now.
> You **drink** it standing up,
> And **leave** the house.

Elma Mitchell has a different way of drawing contrasts by using verb forms. In her poem *Thoughts after Ruskin*, she contrasts Ruskin's *lilies and roses* view of women with her own view, which emphasises the incredible activity and brutal reality of women's lives by using a string of *-ing* participles indicating continuous activity:

> **Gutting** and **stuffing**, **pickling** and **preserving**,
> **Scalding**, **blanching**, **broiling**, **pulverizing**,
> – All the terrible chemistry of their kitchens.

Although this abundance of -*ing* forms is enough to make the point, Mitchell chooses to underline it with a two-line section describing the 'activity' of the women's husbands:

> Their distant husbands **lean** across mahogany
> And delicately **manipulate** the market, . . .

This habitual use of the present tense is so calm and measured amidst the frenzied -*ing*'s of the women, that the men are shown to be doing very little by comparison with their wives.

The technique of creating a 'build-up' of similar verb forms has been used widely, and the outcome differs according to which form is chosen. In *Canticle for Good Friday*, for example, Geoffrey Hill uses a preponderance of past tense forms:

> Thomas (not **transfigured**) **stamped**, **crouched**,
> **Watched**,
> **Smelt** vinegar and blood.

These are only a few of the many past tense verbs to be found in this poem. The finality of simple past tenses as opposed to perfect verb phrases (such as *has stamped*) or progressive forms (such as *was watching*) emphasises Thomas's feeling of hopelessness confronted by Jesus' imminent death. It is further underlined by other -*ed* forms functioning as adjectives: *unsearched, unscratched, untouched*.

Another effect is achieved by using different forms of the same verb. Marge Piercy uses this technique to contrast the process of waking up at different times in her life in her poem *Mornings in various years*:

> **To wake** and see the day piled up
> before me like dirty dishes: . . .

> **Waking** alone I would marshal my tasks . . .

> I **wake** with any two cats, victors
> of the nightly squabble of who
> sleeps where, . . .

Piercy takes us through the process of waking in three different years. The first uses an infinitive to give an endless feeling; this period of life seemed as though the monotony would go on for ever. The use of a present participle -*ing* form at the beginning of the second stanza also implies endlessness, but adds a habitual dimension to the routine. This is emphasised by the phrase *marshal my tasks* which suggests a teeth-gritting determination to be busy and organised. The final stanza introduces a happy period of life in which day begins in friendly chaos in a bed occupied by a partner as well as two cats. The verb in this case is in the present tense and also has a habitual meaning; there is an optimistic feeling that the happiness will continue.

INFORMATION STRUCTURE

English sentences and clauses usually place the focus of the information on the last obligatory clause element. Emphasis can therefore be given to new or important information by making sure that it occurs toward the end of a sentence or clause. In the opening line of *The Hollow Men*, for example, Eliot uses a quite normal order of clause elements:

> Subject: We
> Verb: are
> Complement: the hollow men . . .

The length of the complement here is another indication of its information value in the clause. Subject pronouns (*he*, *she*, *we*, etc.) usually refer to someone or something already known to the reader. Objects, complements and adverbials are more likely to bring new information into the sentence and are therefore also likely to be longer than subjects.

Despite this general tendency, the language has ways of emphasising specific clause elements by moving them to the end of the structure. Auden, for example, places the subject at the end of this sentence from *Musée des Beaux Arts* as well as bringing the adverbial (*about suffering*) to the beginning:

> About suffering they were never wrong,
> The Old Masters: . . .

The effect is to focus on the *Old Masters* whose work the poem considers.

This kind of inversion, where the full subject is delayed and needs to be replaced by a pronoun (*they* in this case) is rather formal in its effect and, for this reason perhaps, is found less often in this century than previously. Other changes in information structure, however, have become more common.

More 'natural-sounding' (i.e. more like spoken style) inversions come from changing the positions of the subject and the complement in a clause with *be* (or similar verb) as the main verb. In everyday speech we are as likely to say *The victims were the police* as *The police were the victims*. The opening of *Thrushes* is a poetic example, although the complement in this case is an adjective, not a noun phrase: *Terrifying are the attent, sleek thrushes on the lawn*. Here Hughes has 'fronted' the complement, *terrifying*, and postposed the subject, *the attent, sleek thrushes*. As well as focusing the information on the subject, this particular inversion achieves a force in the poem's opening word which echoes its meaning, producing a fear analogous to that produced by the birds themselves.

Another way of moving clause elements without making the structure too formal is to move optional adverbials. These are the kind of adverbials which could be deleted from a clause without making it ungrammatical and are fairly flexible in their position in the clause. The adverbials in brackets could be deleted from the following (invented) example with loss of information but leaving a grammatical and understandable clause: (At six o'clock) he (suddenly) started to dance (on a table). Some poets place these adverbials in slightly unusual positions to create particular effects. The following extract comes from *Canticle for Good Friday* by Geoffrey Hill:

> While the dulled wood
> Spat **on the stones** each drop
> Of deliberate blood.

Here, the adverbial of place (*on the stones*) would probably more usually come at the end of the sentence but this would have undermined the end-focus on the object (*each drop of deliberate blood*) which is made doubly effective by the alliteration of the /d/ sound.

This section has illustrated a relatively normal manipulation of information structure, similar to that used in ordinary conversation for emphasis. Other examples, more symbolically related to the meaning of the poems, are found in the next section.

SYMBOLIC GRAMMAR

Although the English language is relatively inflexible in its word order and inflections, poets throughout the ages have found ways of making the syntax reflect their meaning in some way. The twentieth century is no exception to this and, if anything, has been more daring than previous eras in its exploitation, and even violation, of grammatical rules.

'Ungrammaticality' is a difficult concept to define; how many of us, for example, speak in complete sentences? However, poets have traditionally adhered to the rules of the written language and have shied away from constructions that would be considered 'wrong' by purists. In this century, partly as a result of the attention to spoken language mentioned earlier, there have been more minor sentences (sentences without a verb) and other grammatical surprises than ever before. The following excerpt from *Downpour*, by Penelope Shuttle, for example, was discussed in chapter 2. It has two sentences, neither of which has a main verb, although the first has three participles (*blown*, *seeping* and *helped*) and one finite verb (*comes*) all occurring in subordinate clauses:

> Through the letter box, leaves instead of letters,
> wet leaves blown along the path
> and seeping through the low letter box,
> an invasion that comes slowly,
> but helped by the rain. The downpour.

Ungrammaticality in poetry tends to be mainly syntactic (i.e. concerned with the arrangement of words). There have been a few poets in the twentieth century, however, who have experimented with the structures of words themselves, their morphology. The most obvious example of this experimentation comes from the work of e.e. cummings. We have already encountered his poem *love is more thicker than forget*, where cummings rejects the normal way of constructing comparative adjectives in English. In other poems he plays with derivational processes, producing words such as *undeath* and *spaceful* (from *the great advantage of being alive*).

Moving away from 'ungrammaticality' we find that other poets have made symbolic use of optional syntactic features to emphasise their point. Louis MacNeice, for example, has a poem about a lonely and unloved *clerk* sitting alone in the park and acutely conscious of the apparent sexual and social success of everyone and everything around him (*The Lake in the Park*). The list of sights which rub salt in the wound for MacNeice's character are not conjoined, as they might have been, by *and*; the effect is a stark, drumming series of clauses, each underlining the happiness of something in the surroundings:

> On the bank a father and mother goose
> Hiss as he passes, pigeons are courting,
> Everything mocks; the empty deck-chairs
> Are set in pairs, there is no consorting . . .

Another example of conjunctions not being used when they could have been is found at the beginning of Yeats's poem, *The Second Coming*:

> Turning and turning in the widening gyre
> The falcon cannot hear the falconer;
> Things fall apart; the centre cannot hold;
> Mere anarchy is loosed upon the world, . . .

At each of the semi-colons in this extract there is a break between clauses which **could** have been lexically joined by *and*. However, the tone of Yeats's warning about the coming catastrophe is made more serious by the bald statements coming like drumbeats one after the other and the 'pieces' of the stanza symbolise the pieces of a world spinning to destruction.

A different effect is achieved by Marge Piercy in the following example from *In the Men's Room(s)* where there are *and* conjunctions between each pair of clauses:

> They were talking of integrity and existential ennui
> while the women ran out for six-packs **and** had abortions

> in the kitchen **and** fed the children **and** were
>   auctioned off.

The breathless list of what the women were doing while the men talked is enhanced by the style, which is reminiscent of a child's storytelling, piling up clause upon clause. This naivety adds force to the shocking juxtaposition of *had abortions* and *were auctioned off* with other, very mundane activities like shopping and feeding the children.

The final type of symbolic use of grammar to be illustrated here is the use of what we could call 'delaying tactics' in the structure of a clause. We have already seen that early parts of the clause (subject and early adverbials) tend to be short, allowing the information-carrying larger elements to occur in focused positions after the verb. As a result of this general tendency, the reader/hearer of an English sentence has a feeling of anticipation leading up to the verb phrase, which gives way to a kind of down-hill momentum after the verb phrase is reached. It is more difficult to understand a sentence which delays the verb phrase than one which has an early verb phrase. Compare, for example, the following invented sentences where the main verb is in bold type:

> The man in the green coat by the door who was just
> talking to the woman with the red hat **is** my brother.
> My brother **is** the man in the green coat by the door
> who was just talking to the woman with the red hat.

In everyday conversation we usually try to make our sentences easy to understand by avoiding the delay of the verb. However, poetry has both a communicative and an aesthetic function to fulfil and sometimes uses the possibility of delay to parallel in the structure the meaning of the sentences.

The two most obvious ways of delaying the verb phrase in a sentence are first, to put a very long adverbial, or string of adverbials, in front of the subject, and secondly, to create an unusually long subject. The first kind of delay is illustrated from *Dulce et Decorum Est* by Wilfred Owen:

> Dim, through the misty panes and thick green light,
> As under a green sea, I saw him drowning.

Here, the three adverbials (*dim, through* . . . and *As* . . .) delay the start of the main part of the clause and create a feeling of antici- pation, symbolising the kind of slow-motion vision Owen had of the man he watched gassed to death in front of his eyes.

The second kind of delay, the long subject, can be seen in Philip Larkin's poem *Broadcast*, which is analysed in detail in chapter 8. Larkin also uses a delaying tactic, this time after the verb, in the poem *VI* from *The North Ship*:

> Prolong the talk on this or that excuse,
> Till the night comes to rest
> While some high bell is beating two o'clock.

Here the verb comes first in the form of a command: *Prolong*. It is followed by a symbolic 'prolonging' of the sentence itself in the form of three adverbials (*on* . . . , *Till* . . . and *While* . . .). In con- trast to the anticipation noted in the previous example, we feel here the decline in the quality of the conversation which has been to, and past, its main focal point (symbolically the verb) and is running down fast, but the participants still do not want to stop.

7 Textual Cohesion and Orientation

COHESION

A text, whether it is a newspaper article, a novel, a personal letter, a telephone conversation or a poem, is not just a random series of sentences; there are structural and semantic connections between the sentences of a text which help to create its coherence. The term *cohesion* refers to this interconnectedness of sentences in texts.

Let us consider, for example, the opening sentences of A. Alvarez's Introduction in the anthology of poetry edited by him and called *The New Poetry* (1962):

> In 1932 F.R. Leavis proclaimed that Eliot and Pound had between them brought about a significant reorientation of literature. Twenty years later he took most of it back again. . . .

The two sentences here are firstly connected by time; the adverbial *Twenty years later* in sentence 2 relates back to the adverbial *In 1932* from sentence 1. They are also connected by pronominal reference; *he* refers back to *F.R. Leavis* and *most of it* refers back to Leavis's proclamation about Eliot and Pound.

Note that these cohesive *ties* between sentences are not the only clues to the meaning of texts. The same items used here for cohesive effect may, in other texts, be used to refer **outside** the text, to something in the situational context. So, pronouns may be used in the absence of fuller references, to refer to someone whose identity is known to both speaker/writer and hearer/reader. Take the

114

example of a personal letter between friends about a third friend, a boyfriend perhaps. The writer may not want to name *him*, but may safely say **He** *phoned me three times this week!* Adverbials, even relative ones like *later*, can also be used situationally: *I'll see you later* spoken to someone's face has no connection within the text but is intended to mean *later than now* and is usually understood as such.

To return to cohesive ties, there are a number of ways in which texts are 'knitted together'. We have mentioned chronological sequence in the example above, but there can also be logical sequences, introduced, for example, by *therefore* and causal sequences introduced by conjunctions such as *as a result*:

> I think. Therefore I am. (Descartes)
>
> I fell over. As a result I twisted my ankle.

Pronominal reference, also mentioned above, provides much of the economy of the language (pronouns prevent a great deal of repetition) as well as tying texts closely together.

The vocabulary of a text also provides many cohesive ties through such devices as the use of synonyms, opposite meanings, lexical fields and collocations. Many of the examples discussed in chapter 5 provide cohesive ties between the sentences of the poem concerned. Here we will consider just two examples, showing opposition and lexical fields in operation as cohesive devices. The first example comes from the opening of the third part (III) of Harrison's poem *Illuminations*:

> The family didn't always feel **together**.
> Those silent teas with all of us **apart**. . . .

The words in bold type make a formal connection between the two sentences by means of their semantic relationship; they are opposites. The poignant atmosphere is emphasised by the fact that the family are clearly *together* physically at the *silent teas*, but are quite distant emotionally. This common theme of Harrison's work is explored further in the rest of the poem.

The second example of cohesion through vocabulary is similar to the discussion in chapter 5 of Larkin's poem *Water* where there are two interwoven lexical fields running throughout the poem. In the present example, *Wind*, by Ted Hughes, there are three main groups of words which are clustered around the semantic fields of sight, sound and movement. This fairly short poem of six four-line stanzas describes in vivid terms a night and day of stormy wind in a country house: *This house has been far out at sea all night.* The poem is woven tightly together by the members of the three semantic fields. The groups are as follows:

Sound	Sight	Movement	
crashing	blinding	stampeding	wielded
booming	lens	floundering	flung
drummed	mad eye	rose	
bang	look up	new places	dented
rang	balls of eyes	scaled	bent
cry out	grimace	move	shatter
hearing	vanish	strained	
	watch	quivering	grip
	seeing	flap	sit on
		tremble	

It is clear from these groups that the cohesion of the text rests extensively on the structure of the vocabulary. However, these groups are neither clear-cut nor water-tight. So, for example, some of the 'sound' words (*crashing*, *drummed*) may also indicate movement. Equally some of the movement words (*stampeding*, 'flap') have connotations concerned with sound. The three small groups in the righthand column are related to the movement verbs in the following ways: *wielded* and *flung* involve an agent, someone who causes the movement of something else. *Dented*, *bent* and *shatter* also involve an agent, but this time the movement causes a change in the shape of the object: *the brunt wind that dented the balls of my eyes*. Finally, *grip* and *sit on* imply a **lack** of movement, opposites to the main group in a way. But they share a determination not to move, a resistance to the general chaos around and are therefore more concerned with movement than the verbs *rest* or *stay still*, for example, would be. The last aspect of these semantic fields to notice is that the largest group, concerned with movement, progresses from large, uncontrolled movements (*stampede*, *floundering*) to smaller and more

restrained ones (*quivering* and *tremble*). This progression reflects
the moving focus of the poem, from the woods and hills, via the
outside of the house, to the fireside, where the inhabitants try to
escape the worst effects of the wind.

One aspect of cohesion which is the special province of poetry is
the use of sound to tie a text together. The usual devices of sound
as described in chapter 3 (alliteration, assonance, rhyme, rhythm,
syllabics and stresses or metre) can all contribute to the cohesiveness of poetic texts, but are relatively little used in other kinds of
texts. To illustrate the relevance of sound to cohesion, let us consider the first stanza of *Upper Lambourne*, by John Betjeman:

> Up the ash-tree climbs the ivy,
>   Up the ivy climbs the sun,
> With a twenty-thousand pattering
>   Has a valley breeze begun,
> Feathery ash, neglected elder,
>   Shift the shade and make it run – ...

This excerpt illustrates the regular, formal features of sound
patterning in a poem. There are six lines of alternating 8 and 7
syllables, each with four main stresses occurring at regular
intervals. The second, fourth and sixth lines also rhyme. This
pattern continues virtually unchanged throughout the remaining
three stanzas of the poem and is one of the signals that this is,
indeed, a text.

At the other extreme from Betjeman's poetry, we find free
verse with no formal or regular features of sound at all. However,
alliteration and assonance, if used widely throughout a poem,
sometimes contribute to the total cohesive effect. These effects
have already been described in detail in chapter 3.

Sequence and Reference

It remains to investigate the cohesive uses of sequence and
reference in poetry of the twentieth century. We should note,
first of all, that where poetry uses cohesive devices in exactly the
same way as any other text, it is least interesting to us. We simply
notice that very often, chronological sequence or pronominal
reference works normally. Ted Hughes's poem *View of a Pig*, for

example, opens with two sentences connected by normal pronoun reference:

> The pig lay on a barrow dead.
> It weighed, they said, as much as three men.

Here the pig of the first sentence is referred to by the pronoun *it* in the second. Note also that the most common order for the two parts of a cohesive *tie* is adhered to in this example. The fuller, self-explanatory part (*the pig*) comes first and the referring part (*it*) comes second, referring backwards in the text to its partner. This direction of reference is known as *anaphoric*, the rarer *cataphoric* reference occurs when the order is reversed and the referring word or phrase is followed by the fuller, explanatory part of the tie.

The sequencing of many poems of the twentieth century, whether chronological, logical or causal, is normal. It can, however, form an important part of the poem's message and/or structure, particularly if the sequencing adverbials are placed at the beginning of stanzas or sections as in Marge Piercy's poem *In the Men's Room(s)*. In this poem, Piercy is recording her decline from high optimism in the pursuit of women's equality to complete hopelessness and cynicism. She takes us from youthful naïvety through the realisation that despite her superficial acceptance by the men, her apparent independence made her an object of sexual attention, to her final abandonment of the *men's room* in favour of the kitchen, women's company and women's activities. She shows the passing of time by the initial adverbials of each section which are: *When I was young . . .*, *Eventually I realised . . .* and *Now. . . .*

Although many poems use cohesive devices in an unremarkable way, there are some conventions which distinguish poetic texts from others. One such convention, which is not peculiar to the twentieth century, is the use of the pronoun *you* in the absence of any identifying name. This use of *you* is almost always assumed to be addressed to someone loved by the poet (or narrator, if their identities are separate). One contemporary example (from among many) is Vivienne Finch's poem *Green Ice*:

> what fresh green does my heart mint
> to be finger-smudged   by you
>   across my breasts . . .

A relatively recent variation of this use of unidentified reference is the introduction, into feminist poetry particularly, of *you* referring to a child. In *The Lost Baby Poem*, for example, Lucille Clifton addresses an aborted baby with: *you would have been born into winter* and Sylvia Plath's *Morning Song* celebrates birth with: *Love set you going like a fat gold watch.*

A further cohesive use of pronouns, also more common in the twentieth century than previously, is where the title of the poem contains the explicit reference and the body of the poem refers back to the title using a repeated pronoun. One example of this phenomenon is *Ambulances* by Larkin, where the ambulances are never mentioned in the poem itself, but are referred to only by *they* in the poem. The effect is to enhance the mystique surrounding these morbidly fascinating vehicles, which people stare at, but do not wish to ride in. *The Messenger* by Frances Horovitz is a poem about an old Thracian custom of sacrificing a man to their gods. Throughout the poem, the messenger is referred to simply as *he*. The identity of the sacrificed man, of course, is irrelevant here, and different each year. There is a similar universal relevance in Crichton Smith's poem, *Old Woman*, where the protagonist, doomed to an undignified and slow death, is *she*.

A final example in this section illustrates a further step along the same path, where synonymous words and phrases, some of them quite elaborate, may be used instead of pronouns to form a cohesive chain, connecting the body of a poem with its title. The example comes from *Moon Landing* by W.H. Auden. Having revealed the subject matter of his poem in the title, Auden refers to it subsequently through the poem by the following string of phrases:

> so huge a phallic triumph
> an adventure / it would not have occurred to women /
> think worthwhile
> the deed
> it
> A grand gesture
> this landing . . .

While he uses the pronoun *it* twice, and a fairly straightforward cohesive phrase, *this landing*, Auden also paraphrases the title with phrases which display his contempt for the human achievement which the politicians and media were celebrating rather loudly at the time the poem was written. The *phallic* of the first phrase and the subordinate clause denying women's part in the event in the second extract both show that Auden saw the moon landing as a *macho* display of male supremacy. The phrase *a grand gesture* also undermines the event by bringing to mind other phrases such as *empty gesture*. Circumlocutions of this kind are often seen as belonging to a pompous style and this serves Auden's purpose very well, since he manages both to undermine the moon landing and to mimic some of the pomp used to celebrate it.

Unusual Use of Cohesion in Poetry

Although much of the cohesion in poetry is unremarkable, there are times when poets make effective or surprising use of our expectations about normal texts. One way of being mildly different is to catch and retain the reader's attention by the use of cataphoric reference. As explained above, cataphoric reference uses the linking word (such as a pronoun) first, leaving its precise identity to the explanatory word or phrase in the next clause or sentence. Tony Harrison uses this technique in the opening lines of his poem about the death of his mother, *Book Ends – I*:

> Baked the day she suddenly dropped dead
> we chew it slowly that last apple pie.

Here, the unspoken object of *baked* and the unknown referent of *it* are revealed at the end of the sentence, in focal position: *that last apple pie*. The effect is to draw our attention to the poignancy of eating the pie after she had died. The long, slow revelation of what had been baked also serves to symbolise the difficulty of chewing this pie while the throat is full of emotion.

Another example of cataphoric reference making the reader wait for the identity of a pronoun comes from Thom Gunn's poem *On the Move*:

> On motorcycles, up the road, **they** come:
> Small, black, as flies hanging in heat, **the Boys** . . .

Here the suspense created by this device symbolises the approach of the motorcycles and the gradual identification of their riders. It also hints at the intimidation felt by onlookers observing such a gang.

More common than cataphoric reference is the tendency for poets to make their work less cohesive than would normally be required for a text which is to be read by strangers. This has the effect of making the readers feel included in the action, because the language implies that they already know some of the situational background to which the poem refers. An example of this comes from Larkin's poem *XXX* from *The North Ship*: *So through that unripe day you bore your head*. This opening line has two potentially cohesive words which are, however, unresolved textually. The conjunction *So* is unusually placed in the opening sentence of a text, since it implies a causal relationship with something that has gone before:

I was tired. So I went to bed.

The demonstrative *that*, similarly implies that we have some knowledge of the day which is being discussed. Both of these words fail to tie up elsewhere in the text and the effect is that we, the readers, are included in the private world of the poem although we are, at least at the start of the poem, ignorant of the significance of the day concerned.

One of the results of such a lack of cohesiveness is that the reader, who normally works on the assumption that any series of sentences is a cohesive text, looks for the missing information and makes the connections that are lacking in the text. At its most extreme, the lack of cohesive ties may result in an apparent non-sequitur, as, for example, in Harrison's poem, *Them & [uz]*. After a line quoted from a schoolmaster comes a line of narrative which has no formal link with what has gone before:

'Can't have our glorious heritage done to death!'
I played the Drunken Porter in *Macbeth* . . .

The conclusions the reader is clearly meant to draw are that the teacher has acted on his declared prejudice against Harrison's Yorkshire accent and given him only a minor, and incoherent, part in the school production. These conclusions are based on pragmatic, social and cultural knowledge; the shared knowledge of many British citizens (and probably others too). They are not based on any textual evidence at all.

Not all non-cohesive texts rely on shared knowledge for their interpretation. Although a certain kind of shared knowledge about the Ancient World and classical literature would be useful in interpreting *The Waste Land* (T.S. Eliot), for example, there are many examples of lack of cohesion in this poem which constantly frustrate the reader's attempts to make textual sense of it. Perhaps the most difficult thread to work out in the poem is the referent of *I*. This pronoun refers to a number of different characters, of both sexes, and it is usually only after the switch that we realise the referent has changed, if indeed it has. The *I* of *I read, much of the night* (l. 18), *I was neither/ Living nor dead* (ll. 39–40), *There I saw one I knew* (l. 69) and *Sweet Thames, run softly, till I end my song* (l. 183) may, or may not, be the same as *I, Tiresias* (l. 218). The uncertain and fluctuating identity of people was, of course, a major concern early in the century, and by manipulating the cohesion of his text, Eliot manages to arouse in the reader some of the anxiety he feels.

As a contrast, the next two examples exploit cohesion by using fewer pronouns than expected and yet they have a similar effect to Eliot's portrayal of the complexities of personality. In her poem *The Woman in the Ordinary,* Piercy repeats the phrase *The woman* three times, instead of using the pronoun *she*: *The woman in the ordinary pudgy downcast girl, The woman in the block of ivory soap, The woman of the golden fleece.* We would normally assume that she is writing about three different and contrasting women. But it also seems likely that she is trying to express the idea that women necessarily have to develop a number of different personalities to cope with the varying demands of their oppressed lives.

Similarly in cummings' poem which begins *anyone lived in a pretty how town*, he introduces three potentially different sets of characters called *anyone, someones* and *everyones*. His creative use of these general pronouns as proper names is slightly confusing, but more problematic is the question of whether they refer to the same person, or to different people. The answer is in the story of the poem which describes the progress of *anyone* from lonely isolation, through the discovery of love whereupon they become *someones* (in the eyes of the world) to the point when they marry their *everyones* (i.e. they are everyone to each other).

The final example of unusual exploitation of cohesive potential in poetry is from a poem by Adrian Henri called *The New, Fast, Automatic Daffodils*. Here, Henri uses two cohesive texts, Wordsworth's poem about daffodils and a Dutch motor-car advertising leaflet. He intermingles the two until he achieves a third, fully cohesive text promoting a new car called the Daffodil:

> 10,000 saw I at a glance
> Nodding their new anatomically shaped heads in
>   sprightly dance
> Beside the lake beneath the trees
> in three bright modern colours . . .

Mitchell's experiment illustrates the tendency of texts to resolve themselves in the reader's mind into a coherent and cohesive form, however they are constructed.

ORIENTATION

This section introduces a type of categorisation that is more general than much of the analysis in this book. It could have been headed 'Rhetoric' or 'Sub-genres', but these terms have many different uses and were considered to be too confusing. Instead, what we are considering here can be seen as the general *orientation* of the poem; who it addresses, whether it describes a scene, recounts a tale and so on. Clearly, many poems may have more than one of these orientations. The purpose in this section is to introduce archetypal poetic orientations so that the reader can make judgements about more complicated examples by comparing them to the poems discussed here.

The first type of orientation discussed here is one that occurs quite frequently in twentieth-century poetry; poems written in the second person, that is, addressed to 'you'.[1] It is apparent that the identity of this directly addressed audience ranged very widely and is not at all restricted to the 'beloved' of traditional love poetry.

In fact, although 'traditional' poetry is very often addressed to the lover, there were also a few other types of addressee before 1900. The next few paragraphs outline the situation before this century, so that clearer comparisons can be made.

In the seventeenth century, John Donne wrote a number of poems addressed to his lover of the time. These included the Love Elegies *His Picture*, *On his Mistris* and *To his Mistris Going to Bed* and many others including *The Flea*, *The Good-Morrow* and *Aire and Angels* (Gardner, 1957). He is not alone among the Metaphysical poets in writing much of his poetry as if it were a letter to his beloved. In the same collection, Andrew Marvell tries to tempt his lover into bed in *To his Coy Mistris* as does Thomas Carew less famously in *Perswasions to enjoy*. But was the lover the only direct addressee of seventeenth-century poetry? No: the other main recipient of poetry written in the second person was God. There are many examples that could be cited, but George Herbert was perhaps the most consistent writer of such poems; the Penguin collection (Gardner, 1957) contains eight addressed directly to God (or Jesus Christ), although the remainder of the twenty-four by Herbert are also religious in theme.

The eighteenth century saw a shift in the addressees of second-person poetry. Although love poetry continues (e.g. Samuel Johnson: *To Miss Hickman Playing on the Spinet* and *The Winter's Walk*), poetry began to have a new social and political role which led Swift to write *To Their Excellencies the Lords Justices of Ireland*, a poem describing the story of a young woman robbed of her dowry which is written as a letter asking for money. We also find Oliver Goldsmith writing a poem in reply to an invitation in *Verses in Reply to an Invitation to Dinner at Dr Baker's*. The incoming Romantic movement meant that the late eighteenth century saw poems written in response to personal emotions and recollections and this gave rise to second-person poetry addressed both to familiar landscapes and to human emotions. The first of these is found in Thomas Gray's *Ode on a Distant Prospect of Eton College* which speaks to *ye distant spires*, *Ah happy hills* and *Say Father Thames*. The second type of addressee (emotion) was a favourite of William Collins (among others) who wrote Odes *to Pity*, *to Fear*, *to Liberty*, *to Mercy* and *to Simplicity*.

When the Romantic period was in full swing, the number of poems addressed to natural phenomena increased quite rapidly; William Blake wrote *To the Evening Star*, Robert Burns wrote *Ye Flowery Banks* in which he addresses the birds, Leigh Hunt wrote to *The Grasshopper and the Cricket*, Percy Bysshe Shelley wrote variously to *The Moon* and *The Nile* and John Keats wrote to a *Nightingale*, *Autumn* and *Ailsa Rock* respectively.,

Although the twentieth century has poems written to similar groups of second-person addressees, it has added at least one major group and has varied the attitude displayed to the most traditional group of addressees, the lovers.

There are, of course, still poems written to extol the virtues of a beloved as, for example, *The Confirmation* by Edwin Muir, but they are in a minority amongst poems addressed to lovers. There are others which are poignantly affectionate in describing a relationship that is over. For example, Andrew Motion's *Bathing at Glymenopoulo* is about a prostitute, Charlotte Mew's *In Nunhead Cemetery* is about a dead lover and Mebdh McGuckian's *The Weaver Girl* is written from the perspective of a naïve young woman who has obviously been used by a rich and callous man and is pregnant by him, but seems to feel no anger towards him, even though she is denied his company and his support.

Apart from praise and nostalgia, other attitudes towards the lover vary as widely as people's experience and yet there are recognisable groups of addressees within the poems. There are, for example, those which reveal a cooling off of the relationship such as Wendy Cope's *Depression*. Auden's *Lay your sleeping head my love . . . .* illustrates another kind of love poem, common in the uncertain period around and between the two world wars, which doubts the all-conquering power of love, while clinging to it as the only comfort left.

> Lay your sleeping head, my love,
> Human on my faithless arm; . . .

In the tradition of such poetry, Auden makes much of the passage of time and encroaching old age and death. Like Marvell and Donne in the sixteenth century he too urges forgetfulness in the joy of love:

> But in my arms till break of day
> Let the living creature lie,
> Mortal, guilty, but to me
> The entirely beautiful.

Other twentieth-century poems seem to reflect some of the traditional modes of feeling in love poetry, such as distress at parting from, or absence of the object of love: Anne Ridler's *At Parting* and Michael Longley's *Swans Mating*. There are poems addressed to ex-lovers as in Edna St Vincent Millay's *Passer Mortuus Est* and *Sonnet xxiv*, and poems written to the lover, but whose subject-matter is not the relationship itself. The last group includes Philip Larkin's *Lines on a Young Lady's Photograph Album* where the interest of the writer is taken up at least as much by the value and effects of photographic records as by the 'young lady' herself. Amongst many poems which reflect the twentieth-century dissatisfaction with permanent relationships there are also a few poems addressed to partners in stable married relationships, placing value on the friendship and companionship such relationships can bring. These include Rosemary Dobson's *The Fever* where a woman ill in bed wonders what the depth of her husband's empathy for her is, and Christopher Reid's *Parable of Geometric Progression* which focuses on the domestic ritual of untangling the washing and its significance in the relationship concerned.

An investigation of poetry prior to 1900 revealed a few cases of poems addressed to friends and relatives. The twentieth century has taken up this option widely and there are many poems written to specific individuals in the writer's (or narrator's) family or specific friends of the writer. Some examples are Tony Harrison's *Book Ends* addressed to his dead father and *Timer* to his dead mother, Jane Cooper's *El Sueño de la Razón* addressed to a cousin, Adrienne Rich's *Snapshots of a Daughter-in-Law* and John Holloway's *Warning to a Guest*. Jane Cooper's poem, for example, dedicated to 'C. in a mental hospital' opens with a direct address to the person concerned:

> Cousin, it's of you I always dream
> as I walk these dislocated lawns . . .

Her poem, however, also manages to address a theme which is of interest to the unknown reader. Indeed, it is unlikely that the original addressee was really intended to receive the poem; the letter style is simply a way of broaching the difficult subject of mental illness and the definition of sanity.

Where the twentieth century departs from poetry of previous eras is in addressing poems directly not just to individuals, but to groups of people, some of them very wide such as all men/boys (Carol Rumens, *A Poem for Chessmen*), women (Aldous Huxley's *Second Philospher's Song*) and even all the people who love England (Cecil Day Lewis's *You That Love England*). The anxiety that goes with uncertainty no longer seems to worry the modern poet who also uses the second person pronoun to address the reader (not knowing who that may be) or some indeterminate person. Stephen Spender's *The Double Shame* is one example of a poem written to a vague addressee while T.S. Eliot's *The Love Song of Alfred J. Prufrock* either addresses an unknown figure or more likely invites the reader to witness the story.

Some poems have political or social messages which are more easily accepted by the reader when they are ostensibly addressed to another person. Such is the case with Mervyn Morris's poem *To an Expatriate Friend* which bemoans the increasing consciousness of skin colour following the rise of the Black Liberation movement. He addresses a friend who has presumably gone to live away from Morris's native Jamaica. He describes the friend as *colour-blind* because prior to the 'revolution' he took no notice of people's skin colour, but at the end of the poem he says:

> It hurt to see you go; but, more,
> it hurt to see you slowly going white.

We are never told, but we assume that the friend is also black, although he or she somehow manages to 'join' white society, perhaps by going to England or the USA and doing well while forgetting his or her roots. Whatever the details of the story (it would work as well with a white friend whose whiteness began to show), Morris's poem manages to convey his disappointment at the way that the rise in black consciousness affected relationships. The orientation of the poem as a private letter to a particular friend does not get in the way of this message, but rather makes it all the more poignant.

While the Romantic influence on poetry survives, there will be poems not only about, but addressed to, the natural world. In fact, this kind of addressee is poorly represented in the twentieth century, although there is, for example, D.H. Lawrence's *The*

Mosquito, addressed to a mosquito, Anne Stevenson's *Giving Rabbit to my Cat Bonnie* which is addressed to the cat and there are also a number of poems written to shrubs and flowers (e.g. Arthur Waley's *The Chrysanthymums in the Eastern Garden* and Sylvia Plath's *Poppies in July*).

The second main addressee of earlier poetry, namely God, seems to be all but absent in the mainstream of poetry in the twentieth century. There is the occasional poem apparently addressing God, such as Louise Glück's *The Gift* which has a traditional prayer-opening: *Lord*. However, even this poem implies that the writer is not a believer, she simply wishes that her son could believe in miracles. We should not assume that spirituality is therefore absent from the century's poetry. There are many poems addressed to pagan-sounding spirits such as *Deus Loci* (Spirit of Place) as in Lawrence Durrell's poem of the same name and 'Lord of the Images' as in Thomas Blackburn's poem *Hospital for Defectives*. There are also poems that address, for example, the Western Star (Rosemary Dobson's *Country Press*) or the year (Judith Wright's *Request to a Year*) or even 'Mother Toothache' (John Heath-Stubbs' *A Charm against the Toothache*).

Perhaps the most striking change in the addressees of the twentieth century is in the number of poems written to children. Although we might assume that the increase in publication of women's poetry is responsible for this, many poems with this kind of orientation have been written by men. There is a tendency for these poems to look toward the future as in Sassoon's *The Child at the Window* and Robert Graves' *Warning to Children*. This may well be a reaction to the wars of the early part of the century. It is noticeable that the poems written by women are of a much more personal nature and address, for example, a bereaved child (Frances Bellerby's *Bereaved Child's First Night*), an unborn baby (Sylvia Plath's *You're*) and an unknown number of aborted babies (Gwendolyn Brooks' *The Mother*).

It may be the case, that who we write to in the twentieth century at least partly defines who we are. We are no longer in a world where poetry idealises love. Instead we are more often moved to write to those we have failed to love or those who have died and whose only after-life in a godless world is in our memory. It is also an impersonal world in which we try to relate to complete strangers as in Frances Cornford's *To a Fat Lady Seen from the Train* and a world in which the technological complexity surrounding us makes the relatively simple technology of a paper-clip seem attractive and worthy of poetic eulogy (*Ode to a Paperclip* by Douglas Dunn).

Another quite common and fairly simple orientation of poems in this century is the storytelling mode. Although modern poetry has not seen the ballad or long poem as a very important part of its scope since it is now covered in some measure by the novel, there are many short poems which make a philosophical, political or social point by means of a story. Tess Gallagher's *Black Silk*, for example, tells the story of an incident which happened during the mourning period following an old man's (a father's?) death. This particular story is written in the past tense and measures out the distance between the widow and the narrator (the son or daughter perhaps), the latter feeling bereaved but also rather distant from the grief:

> Time
> to go to her, I thought, with that
> other mind, and stood still.

While Gallagher's story focuses on personal grief and individual responses to it, Douglas Dunn's poem *A Removal from Terry Street* makes use of a story to make social comment on the poverty found amongst the working classes in the 1960s. He describes a scene of a family pushing a handcart laden with their belongings: *A mattress, bed ends, cups, carpets, chairs.* The 'story' is factual and realistic since we see the family only while they are in Terry Street; once they have turned the corner we no longer have any information. We are not told where they are moving to, nor whether they are moving up or down the social ladder. However, Dunn draws some pathos from their removal since their belongings include a lawnmower and there is, we are told, no grass in Terry Street. He ends with a wry comment on this symbol of hope: *That man, I wish him well, I wish him grass.*

Dunn's story about Terry Street uses the present tense to create a feeling of immediacy and we also infer from the tense that this story may be a recurrent feature of life there. Other poets use a more straightforward past tense storytelling mode to enhance the distance between the story and the present day. Louis Simpson, for example, tells the story of a black man released from some kind of detention where he hears the condemned prisoners weeping in their cells: *It was cold and all they gave him to wear / was a shirt.* Simpson's poem (*Back in The States*) makes the point that such experiences are very quickly forgotten when better times arrive. He achieves a distancing from the prison by changing to the present towards the end of the poem: *Now here he was, back in the States.*

Although 'letter' poems and 'story' poems abound, there are many poems which fit into neither of these categories. There are, for example, many descriptive poems in the late twentieth century which differ from those of previous times mainly in their subject-matter. The Romantic and even the Victorian poets would often write poems describing Nature, albeit with the intention of making a philosophical point. Modern poets by contrast find material amongst even the most homely and domestic surroundings. Philip Larkin, for example, wrote descriptions of many everyday scenes including a home that has been left empty (*Home is so sad*) and *Ambulances*. Like the Romantic poets before him, Larkin's descriptive work concealed philosophical foundations. *Ambulances*, for example, is a poem which addresses the problem of facing up to our mortality while *Home is so sad* remarks on the passing of time and the failing of optimism. Anne Stevenson also uses the descriptive orientation to make social comment in her poem *By the Boat House, Oxford*. She describes a scene in which *nice women* are seen with their husbands and sons:

> Their husbands are plainly superior with them,
>> without them.
> Their boys wear privilege like a clear inheritance,
>> easily.

Stevenson's point in describing the scene is to focus on the women and to ask whether they are happy with lives in which they are clearly oppressed. The scene she describes is static, almost like a photograph. This enables the readers to take their time and consider whether the 'nice' women are in fact colluding in their own predicament or not.

While descriptive poetry is one way of focusing on more

abstract or philosophical ideas, some poems address more directly
the moral or political question under consideration. These more
direct attacks on usually controversial issues have arisen most
commonly among writers who have felt themselves to be
oppressed. There are many examples of poems by women and
black writers which use a kind of personal testimony format to
make their point. These are reminiscent of religious testimonies
which often have three parts to them; how I was when a sinner,
the moment of revelation, and how I am now I have 'seen the
light'. One poem which follows this format very closely is *In the
Men's Room(s)* by Marge Piercy. This poem has been discussed at
various points throughout the book, but here it is relevant to
remind the reader of the first line of each of the three stanzas
which are:

> When I was young I believed in intellectual
>   conversation
>
> Eventually of course I learned how their eyes
>   perceived me
>
> Now I get coarse when the abstract nouns start
>   flashing . . .

These three lines illustrate well the **past (sinner) + revelation +
present (saved)** format of the testimony. Other poems are not
so clearly divided into sections, but have a general tone of
pride in their declarations which often have a confessional
element to them. Erica Jong, for example, admits *I am woman
enough / to love the kneading of bread*. But she resolutely declares
I write while / the dust piles up showing her determination not to
'love houses better than herself' as her mother and grandmother
did before her.

   Other political poems may lack the testimonial style of these
examples, but may borrow from another religious tradition:
prayer. Some protest poems about slavery or racial oppression
sound very much like hymns or prayers and often use the formula
Let + pronoun which, although usually not directed at a god, has
an echo of such prayers. Julius Lester's poem *On the birth of my
son, Malcolm Coltrane* uses this formula:

Even as we kill,
Let us
not
forget
that it is only so we may be
more human.

There are also poems which rather than borrowing persuasive techniques from religious traditions, bring the rhetoric of politics into poetry. Fleur Adcock, for example, writes *Against Coupling*, an amusing, though fervent defence of sexual self-satisfaction, a subject which suffers from the taint of taboo: *I write in praise of the solitary act*. Her final stanza opens with a call for support in the stand she has taken:

I advise you, then, to embrace it without
encumbrance.

The final category to be discussed here could be labelled 'hypothetical worlds'. There are many poems in the twentieth century which describe an ideal world, a longed-for but retrospective world or a potential but not necessarily ideal alternative world.

The first of these can be illustrated by Dylan Thomas's poem *And Death Shall Have No Dominion* which is a vision of the afterlife conveying Thomas's wish that the dead will at least enjoy freedom from the fear of death. The irony of the poem is its melancholy celebration of aspects of life that the dead can no longer appreciate:

No more may gulls cry at their ears
Or waves break loud on the seashores; . . .

The second hypothetical world is the longed-for return to a previous time. Douglas Dunn has a number of poems that deal with this theme in connection with the death of his wife. Perhaps the most poignant is *Kaleidoscope*:

To climb these stairs again, bearing a tray,
Might be to find you pillowed with your books . . .

The inability to accept the death of someone close to us is aptly conveyed by this replaying of old scenes which will not recur in reality.

The final example is one which describes a potential alternative world, but not one which has any particular advantage over this one. Larkin's poem *Water* has been mentioned in connection with its three interwoven lexical fields. But its overall orientation is one that depends on the conditional clause occupying the first two lines of the poem:

> If I were called in
> To construct a religion . . .

Larkin proceeds to tell us what his religion would be like and we are misled at first into thinking that he is describing a different religion to the familiar one; an ideal religion. In fact, as the poem progresses we become aware that all the symbolism he is using is reminiscent of the world religions, particularly in their use of water. The world-weariness of Larkin's religion is left with the reader as an after-taste following the closing lines of the poem whose choice of the mundane *endlessly* instead of the euphoric *eternally* sums up the hopelessness he feels:

> Where any-angled light
> Would congregate endlessly.

8 Examples of Analysis

A HAIRLINE FRACTURE by Amy Clampitt

1   Whatever went wrong, that week, was more than weather:
       a shoddy streak in the fabric of the air of London
       that disintegrated into pollen
       and came charging down by the bushelful,
5   an abrasive the color of gold dust, eroding
       the tearducts and littering the sidewalks
       in the neighborhood of Sloane Square,

       where the Underground's upper reaches have the
                                                                 character,
       almost, of a Roman ruin – from one
10   crannied arcade a dustmop of yellow blossom
       hung with the stubborn insolence of the unintended,
       shaking still other mischief from its hair
       onto the platform, the pneumatic haste of missed
       trains, the closing barrier –

15   wherever we went, between fits of sneezing we quarreled:
       under the pallid entablatures of Belgravia,
       the busy brown façades that were all angles
       going in and out like a bellows, even the small house
       on Ebury Street where Mozart, at the age of eight,
20   wrote his first symphony, our difference
       was not to be composed.

       Unmollified by the freckled plush of mushrooming
       monkeyflowers in the windowboxes of Chelsea, undone
       by the miraculous rift in the look of things
25   when you've just arrived – the remote up close,

134

the knowing that in another, unentered existence
everything shimmering at the surface is this minute
merely, unremarkably familiar –

it was as though we watched the hairline fracture
30   of the quotidian widen to a geomorphic fissure,
its canyon edge bridged by the rainbows of a terror
that nothing would ever again be right
between us, that wherever we went, nowhere
in the universe would the bone again be knit
35   or the rift be closed.

This poem illustrates many of the techniques and effects discussed
in chapters 2–7. Most of the technical vocabulary used here should
be familiar, but the glossary should be used in cases of doubt.
Although the following discussion largely follows the order of the
other chapters, in analysing a complete poem there are times
when a more integrated approach is appropriate.

The first thing to notice about this poem is that the sound
effects are not those of traditional rhyme and metre. There is no
regular end-rhyme (or even half-rhyme). There is no obvious pattern of syllables (the lines range between 6 and 14 syllables in
length) and there is no regular metre; stresses per line vary
between 3 and 6.

However, the lack of musical form does not imply that there is
no music in the poem. Clampitt relies on alliteration, assonance
and internal rhyme for her sound effects. There are, for example,
a number of sequences of /w/ alliteration:

Whatever went wrong, that week, was more than
        weather: . . .

This opening line is full of the semi-vowel /w/ which lacks the
force of stronger consonants such as plosives (e.g. /t/, /d/, /k/)
and lends itself to symbolising the stifling heat and oppressive relationship which are the subjects of the poem. This consonant recurs
in line 15 (*wherever we went*) and also throughout the final stanza
(*we watched / widen / rainbows / would ever / between us / wherever we went, nowhere / would the bone . . .*).

Interspersed with these heavy but imprecise consonants are the many sibilant sounds used to indicate the sporadic sneezing of the quarrelling lovers, both afflicted by hay fever. Almost every line contains some /s/ (and other sibilant) sounds, but a few examples will convey the idea:

> l.2   a shoddy streak in the fabric of the air of
>   London . . .
> l.10   a dustmop of yellow blossom . . .
> l.13   the pneumatic haste of missed/trains . . .

Other effects are more local. For example, Belgravia is described alliteratively as having *busy brown* façades and its *pallid entablatures* contain the assonance of two /a/ vowels. The first two lines of stanza four have /m/, /l/, /f/ and /ʃ/ alliteration as well as assonance in the shape of a repeated /ʌ/ or /u/ vowel (depending on your accent):

> Unmollified by the freckled plush of mushrooming
> monkeyflowers in the windowboxes of Chelsea,
>   undone . . .

These are probably the most musical lines of the poem and it is clear that in this case the aesthetic effect comes from a build-up of a number of harmonies of sound.

Only one sound effect corresponds to the form of the poem. The first two stanzas and the fourth one do not end with a major grammatical break. Stanza one ends with the adverbial *in the neighborhood of Sloane Square*, which seems finished, but actually continues into stanza two with a relative clause *where*. . . . The last sound of stanza one is an open one /eɜ/ as are the last sounds of stanzas two and four: *barrier* /ɪɜ/ and familiar /ɪɜ/. Stanzas three and five, however, both end with a full-stop and with a plosive consonant:

> 1. 21   composed
> 1. 35   closed.

These are also the only two lines that are end-rhymed and they represent the definite and satisfactory solution of the argument between the protagonists – which will never occur.

One effect in the poem which cuts across the linguistic divisions used in this book is the high number of words containing the negative prefix *un-*:

1. 11	unintended
1. 22	unmollified
1. 23	undone
1. 26	unentered
1. 28	unremarkably

Clearly there is a sound effect here, but the words also have a semantic connection with other negative words which occur in the poem and help to emphasise the negative mood of the couple:

1. 20/1	our difference/was **not** to be composed.
1. 32	that **nothing** would ever again be right
1. 33	between us, that wherever we went,
	nowhere . .

The other noticeable feature of the first four of these words is that they are adjectives derived from verbs (*mollify* → *mollified*) before having the prefix added (i.e. there is no verb *to unmollify*). The transition from verb to adjective perhaps emphasises the lack of action taken by the couple who seem to be helplessly swept along by the inevitable decline of their relationship.

As well as these words, there are a number of other examples of participles (-ing and -en forms of the verb) used sometimes to premodify nouns:

1. 13/14	**missed** trains
1. 14	the **closing** barrier

and sometimes used as the non-finite verb phrase in a clause:

1. 4	**charging** down by the bushelful
1. 5	**eroding** the tearducts
1. 6	**littering** the sidewalks
1. 12	**shaking** still other mischief from its hair
1. 18	**going** in and out like a bellows
1. 27	everything **shimmering** at the surface . . .

These clauses have implicit subjects which are all inanimate, but seem to represent a threat to the people in the poem. First the pollen (first three examples above) then the *busy brown façades* and finally *everything* are the alien phenomena which continuously (continuous participle) challenge the couple. By contrast, the only times when the people themselves form the subject of clauses, they are given simple past tense verb phrases as if to emphasise the discontinuous and stilted nature of their actions:

> 1. 15   wherever we **went**, between fits of sneezing
>   we **quarreled** . . .
> 1. 29   it was as though we **watched** the hairline
>   fracture . . .

The syntax of the whole poem reinforces the sense of helplessness mentioned earlier – the feeling that forces outside the couple were going to result in their eventual splitting up. There are only two sentences in the poem, the first ending at the end of stanza three and the second at the end of the poem. The result is that of a piling up of subordinate clauses, each moving the reader forward, but with the unsatisfactory feeling of wondering when the sentence will end. An example of this effect comes from stanza one:

> a shoddy streak in the fabric of the air of London
> that disintegrated into pollen
> and came charging down by the bushelful,
> an abrasive the color of gold dust, eroding
> the tearducts and littering the sidewalks
> in the neighborhood of Sloane Square, . . .

These lines from stanza one consist of two noun phrases in apposition to *weather* in line 1. In other words, they expand the problem with the weather (heat/ high pollen count) until we feel almost stifled ourselves by the lack of main clauses and there is yet another stanza of subordinate clauses to go before the beginning of stanza three brings the relief of a main clause: *between fits of sneezing we quarreled*.

The syntactic structure of stanzas one and three also provides some of the form which we noted as being absent as far as sound (rhyme and metre) was concerned. These stanzas have parallel structures, each beginning with a clause introduced by a *wh-* word which is subsequently expanded in the rest of the stanza. Stanza one begins with *Whatever went wrong* and describes the weather/pollen through the rest of the stanza. Stanza three, on the other hand, opens with *wherever we went* and expands on the notion of place through the stanza, listing some of the places where the couple sneezed and quarrelled.

The structure of the fourth and fifth stanzas is one long sentence, with two long adverbials taking up the whole of stanza four. Again, this gives a feeling of waiting for the main clause which arrives at the beginning of the final stanza: *it was as though we watched the hairline fracture.*

The symbolic effect of such structure is to reflect the feeling of the couple who are slowly and painfully becoming aware that their *difference was not to be composed.* The slight feeling of relief when the main clause starts is betrayed by another long non-finite clause beginning in line 31 and finishing with a greater sense of relief at the end of the poem. This emphasises the irony of such situations where the resolution, even a sad one, comes as a relief after the acrimonious process leading up to separation.

We have seen that this poem works on the levels of sound and syntax; there are also many semantic effects to be noticed. There is one strong lexical field, a number of double meanings, some near-synonymy, use of opposition, collocation, connotation and selectional restrictions.

First, the lexical field is in the general field of geographical terms, specifically (and appropriately) describing the breaking up of the earth. The words in this field are:

1. 5	eroding
1. 24	rift
1. 29	fracture
1. 30	geomorphic fissure
1. 31	canyon
1. 35	rift.

Apart from the repeated use of *rift* at the end of the poem, there is a progression, reflecting the widening of the gap between the lovers, from *erosion*, a slow crumbling of the earth, through *rift* and *fracture* which involve a split, but no separation of the parts, to *fissure* where the parts separate and the split goes deep, and finally to *canyon* which is both deep and wide – and unbridgeable by anything other than a rainbow. This lexical field also provides the context for a metaphorical representation of the Underground train line as a river, the point of connection being the *overground* (i.e. highest) part of the system which operates in the suburbs and which Clampitt describes as: *the Underground's* **upper reaches**.

There are a number of potential ambiguities in the poem, at different linguistic levels. First, there is a pun on two meanings of *composed* in line 21, where the central meaning of *writing music* is implied by references to Mozart but the context provides the interpretation *resolved* or *made up*. Another word which is exploited in two ways is *fracture*. Although it is part of the geographical field mentioned above, it may also apply to broken bones and this meaning is taken up at the end of the poem when the failing relationship is likened to an irreversibly broken bone: *nowhere/in the Universe would **the bone again be knit***.

The next level of ambiguity depends on the contextual interpretation of an unusual collocation: *pneumatic haste* (line 13). The syntactically appropriate interpretation is that the trains are in a hurry (haste) and their doors are pneumatically controlled. But if we notice that the couple miss a number of trains, we suppose that they are running and therefore wheezing as a result of the combination of hot weather and hay fever. The phrase *pneumatic haste* could equally well apply to them.

Other ambiguities arise because of doubts over syntactic structure. The end of stanza two, for example, may correspond to the end of the clause, but the punctuation (a dash) means that we **could** interpret the following adverbial *wherever we went* as belonging to either of the clauses it joins:

> the closing barrier wherever we went
> wherever we went . . . we quarreled . . .

Probably both of these interpretations are relevant.

The use of negative prefixes has already been mentioned, but could be seen semantically as part of a negative accumulation throughout the poem, emphasising the opposition to all things

positive. Another use of opposition occurs in line 25 where there
is an apparently contradictory phrase:

> undone/by the miraculous rift in the look of things
> when you've just arrived – **the remote up close**, . . .

The point of this contradiction is that the visitors to London feel an
unusual combination of familiarity and strangeness. Most people
around the world have ideas about the look of such a famous city,
but would find the real experience rather different from their imag-
ined perception of it. Note that this dislocation of place adds to the
tension between the lovers, who are both strangers in London, and
are therefore compelled to do their sightseeing together.

The lines quoted above contain one of the examples of unusual
collocation in the poem: *miraculous rift*. The adjective *miraculous*
usually premodifies nouns like *escape* or *recovery*, where the connotations are of positive relief and joy. This use of the word, however, while retaining the central meaning which expresses surprise
or astonishment, does not have connotations of relief or joy.
Instead it conveys with extra force the shock of finding London so
different from their expectations.

Another interesting collocation occurs in line 16: *under the*
pallid entablatures of *Belgravia*. The adjective *pallid* is normally
used to describe people's faces when they look unwell. Here, the
narrator, herself unwell, transfers her feeling to the buildings she
observes and implies that the decorative architraves and cornices
are paler than they should be.

A further example of personification occurs in stanza one when
the pollen is portrayed as a huge enemy, ***charging*** *down by the*
bushelful. Here, we could describe the process as a broken selectional restriction, the verb *charge* usually being applied to animate
and wilful subjects such as armies or elephants. The effect is to
humorously emphasise the paranoia of sufferers from hay fever,
faced with hot weather and blossoming trees.

Connotation has been mentioned above in connection with other effects, but there is one word in the poem where connotation
seems to be the main contributor to its meaning:

> 1.22 Unmollified by the freckled **plush** of mush-
>   rooming monkeyflowers . . .

As well as being a very apt description of the *deep pile* on the petals of monkeyflowers, the word *plush* has connotations of luxury (resulting from its frequent collocation with *hotel* and *decor*) and is sometimes used in a derogatory way to sneer at over-indulgent surroundings. It effectively shows the reader how the unhappy, unwell and far-from-home tourists feel when confronted by the cosy luxury of Chelsea homes – particularly since their windowboxes are contributing to the pollen count.

BROADCAST by Philip Larkin

1   Giant whispering and coughing from
     Vast Sunday-full and organ-frowned-on spaces
     Precede a sudden scuttle on the drum,
     'The Queen', and huge resettling. Then begins
5   A snivel on the violins:
     I think of your face among all those faces,

     Beautiful and devout before
     Cascades of monumental slithering,
     One of your gloves unnoticed on the floor
10   Beside those new, slightly-outmoded shoes.
     Here it goes quickly dark. I lose
     All but the outline of the still and withering

     Leaves on half-emptied trees. Behind
     The glowing wavebands, rabid storms of chording
15   By being distant overpower my mind
     All the more shamelessly, their cut-off shout
     Leaving me desperate to pick out
     Your hands, tiny in all that air, applauding.

In analysing the linguistic effects of this poem, we will go through the poem from beginning to end, building up a picture of the way in which the total effect is created.

The first sentence takes up almost the whole of four lines (to *resettling*) and is a very clear example of symbolic syntax as described in chapter 6. There is a very long subject (the whole of the first two lines) which gives the reader a feeling of uneasiness similar to that felt by an audience anticipating the opening of a concert. We get some relief when the verb, *precede*, occurs. But the long object, consisting of a list of three noun phrases, tells us that our wait is not over because all that is happening is a drum roll, the National Anthem and then everyone has to sit down again. Larkin introduces a note of hope at the end of line 4 when he uses an inversion to delay the subject of the next sentence:

> Then begins
> A snivel on the violins: . . .

So we think that after *The Queen* the concert is about to start, but, of course, the orchestra has yet to tune up.

Within the five lines just described syntactically, Larkin uses other effects. The three participial nouns, *whispering, coughing* and *resettling*, are left without articles and the effect is to make them mass nouns, with no distinct boundaries. So, if we compare *and a huge resettling* with Larkin's version, the presence of the indefinite article seems to limit, and therefore decrease, the size.

Line 2 contains two invented compounds, *Sunday-full* and *organ-frowned-on*, which together evoke the large Town Hall where the concert is presumably taking place. Although the later applause indicates that this is probably not a church or cathedral, the awe we might feel, faced with a large building full of people in hushed expectation, is suggested by the religious connotations of *Sunday* and *organ*. The use of *frowned-on* indicates that we may feel small and insignificant in such an atmosphere.

It is interesting to note that Larkin chooses to describe the size of the building using a series of words all partially synonymous with *large*: *Giant, Vast, spaces, huge, monumental*. The phrase in the last line, *all that air*, also belongs to this semantic group. Two of these words deserve a special mention. First, the plural *spaces* is used in preference to the mass noun *space* and is more effective because the plural version is normally restricted to the collocation *open spaces*, describing landscapes or parks. In this context it conjures up the feeling often associated with very large buildings, that they are like the outdoors, but with a roof on. Secondly, *monumental* reminds us of a number of typical collocations such as *monumental error* or *monumental blunder*. The negative connotation thus gives us a hint that Larkin is less than impressed with the music itself; he is only concerned to *be with* the woman who is attending the concert, in spirit at least.

Returning to the first stanza, we find Larkin using alliteration, (the /s/ sound), assonance (the /ʌ/ sound) and sound-symbolism (in *scuttle*) to evoke the drum roll which brings the audience to their feet for the National Anthem. The /sn/ of *snivel* is also sound-symbolic, having 'nasty' associations in a number of words: *sneer, snide, sneaky*. The usual meaning of *child, crying nasally in a whining fashion* is transferred to the unpleasant sound of violins tuning up.

The sentence begun at the end of stanza one continues for four lines into stanza two without further verb phrases. The lack of verbs contributes to a growing sense of time *standing still*; a common impression at classical music concerts and not necessarily implying boredom, just timelessness. However, it may also be seen as revealing yet again Larkin's impatience at the music. This timeless effect is most obvious in the following line: *One of your gloves unnoticed on the floor*. Here, there could have been a verb (*lies* or *is*) after *gloves*, but verbs require tenses and would therefore spoil the 'snapshot' effect of this line.

In the next line there is an apparent contradiction in the description of the woman's shoes as both *new* and *slightly outmoded*. Clearly there is no real contradiction since it is possible to buy new, but old-fashioned shoes. But we glimpse Larkin's fondness of the person concerned through this attention to detail. He also reveals that he too is *dated*, by using the word *outmoded* rather than something more modern. The choice of this word among other synonyms, such as *old-fashioned*, is symbolic.

There is an alternation of long and short sentences in this poem which is continued in stanza two, line 5: *Here it goes quickly dark*. Larkin places the adverbial *quickly* in a legitimate, but slightly unusual place before *dark*. The effect is to symbolise the sudden nightfall by placing the emphasis on a short, mono-syllabic word ending in a sharp plosive consonant: *dark*. The alternative, to finish the sentence with *quickly*, would have far less impact as it has two syllables and ends in a vowel.

The next sentence runs over three lines, the end of each line containing a syntactic element which shows the sense to be unfinished (i.e. run-on lines). Thus the verb *lose* at the end of line 11 requires an object and the adjective *withering* at the end of the next line is clearly premodifying a noun (*leaves*) which opens the following line. The effect, after the short sentence mentioned above, is for the reader to follow Larkin into his reverie, looking out of the window at the winter trees, as he waits for the concert to finish.

The final stanza describes the last, grand crescendo of the concert, followed by the applause. The apparently frenzied nature of the music is carried in the unusual collocation of the adjective *rabid*, which usually modifies animate nouns, with the abstract noun *storms*. The ending of such loud music often leaves a deafening echo in the ear and Larkin describes this effect as *their cut-off shout*. He uses a phrase evocative of the electrical means by which he is listening to the concert (*cut-off*) and also uses a non-musical, human sound, *shout*, to show that he is not particularly impressed by the music itself.

Finally, Larkin reveals his main interest in the broadcast concert, which is to make some contact with the woman in the audience. It is a twentieth-century equivalent to lovers in different parts of the world both looking at the moon in order to feel in closer contact. Larkin exaggerates his ability to hear her hands clapping among all the others and manages to symbolise the release of energy after a great orchestral climax by the slow pace of the three phrases in the last line, separated by commas.

THE FREEDOM WON BY WAR FOR WOMEN
by Carol Rumens

> From hassock, cradle-side and streaming walls
> – The fogs of faith and washday – thin lives beaten
> Blank and hung to weep – the fair are gone.
>
> Raw-fingered saints who've tipped their pedestals
> And dried their hands at Father Empire's yell,
> They chivvy cautious husbands, rebel sons
> With bloodiest white. But they'll take the same
>   poison,
> Hands deft among his axle-trees and shells.
>
> True warriors, they were furnace-forged when bombs
> Jumped roof-high. From tongue to lung the taste
> Of lead rolled death. Massed engines pumped their
>   Somme.

It was a flowering and a laying waste
– Man's skills found shining at the heart of woman,
His vengeance too, expediently unlaced.

This poem explores – and challenges – the frequently asserted notion that the First World War was a turning point in the struggle to win independence for women. The reasons usually given for such an attitude are that it was during the war that women first worked outside the home in large numbers to support the war effort. Much, though not all, of this paid work was in munitions factories and Carol Rumens focuses on this work in her poem.

The poem opens with a long sentence structured to cause anticipation in the reader. This is achieved by the long adverbial beginning the sentence and lasting for two and a half lines which sets the scene for the main clause: *the fair have gone*. The long adverbial also sums up the kind of lives that women were leading prior to the war when they had duties toward the church (represented by *hassock*), children (*cradle-side*) and housework (the *streaming walls* of washday being the worst of this). Rumens draws a parallel between the literal *fog* of washday and the spiritual *fog* in which people automatically attended church, though often with only a vague idea of its significance, or a confused picture of a religion that supported the so-called 'just war'.

The slight discomfort a reader feels in taking so long to arrive at the main clause symbolises the never-ending round of tasks that faced the women of the day. Rumens also uses the image of washing to describe the kind of lives they led: *thin lives beaten blank and hung to weep*. The image of clothes and linen being almost worn through and hung up to drip on the line is effectively transferred to the women. There is also an echo of another familiar phrase in *beaten blank*, which sounds like 'beaten black and blue', although in this case it is the dulling effect of *blank* that is the worst for women's lives.

This poem has a series of strong images which describe women and the change they went through. After the washing analogy, Rumens calls up a familiar Victorian image of the perfect woman seen as a saint, but she undermines the purity of the image by describing them as *raw-fingered*, showing that their purity is tainted by hard physical work. This collocation of a down-to-earth adjective with a 'pure' noun suggests another meaning of the word *saint*: a long-suffering and uncomplaining servant to other people. These two interpretations of the word *saint* are both kept in view as the sentence continues. The relative clause following the word *saints* implies both the first, pure, meaning as it suggests that they were on *pedestals* but have rejected this elevation, and the second, long-suffering meaning as it evokes the vision of a woman drying her hands as she goes to answer the door: *dried their hands at Father Empire's yell.*

The insidious nature of war is underlined in the next line and a half where Rumens reminds us that, even though they did not fight themselves, women were not always the self-righteous protesters we sometimes imagine. Indeed, they would challenge even strange men to go and join up by presenting them with white feathers denoting cowardice, if they seemed to be in the right age range. The use of an apparently contradictory adjective and noun combination, *bloodiest white*, underlines the hypocrisy of their actions since they were recommending these men to go and die or kill, but were not doing so themselves.

An irony, commenting on this situation, is discussed in the next sentence which points out that the women will *take the same poison* as the men while working in the munitions factories. The fact that the women are both in as much danger and as implicated in the war as the men is underlined by the description of them as *true warriors* in the next sentence. The following image is one that both evokes the factories in which they worked and suggests that they have been through a melting-down process in order to turn them into something new: *they were furnace-forged when bombs jumped roof-high.* This change, according to Rumens, dates from the falling of bombs; she is perhaps suggesting that to live through such fear and horror is bound to change people. As well as the fiery sounds of the alliteration in *furnace-forged*, this image has suggestions of a more ominous nature. Most factory processes involving melted-down metal then go on to use moulds producing a number of identical items at the end of the process. This hint at the anonymous, identical women produced by the war machine is quite frightening.

An internal rhyme, *tongue* and *lung*, in the next sentence has the effect of making the tongue self-conscious, particularly as it is followed by the liquid consonants /l/ and /r/ in *the taste of lead rolled death*. The effect of this use of sound is to make readers feel the taste of lead on their tongues.

The fact that women as well as men were 'pumped full of lead' is finally driven home by the contrastingly short sentence *massed engines pumped their Somme*. The use of the verb *pump* connotes the colloquial phrase quoted above which is used to describe shooting people with machine guns. In the case of the women, it is the factory machines that are pumping and the lead is breathed in from the air rather than shot in the shape of bullets. The devastating effect on life and health, it is suggested, is the same for both.

The last stanza comments on the whole episode in women's history, using the contrasting metaphors of natural abundance (*flowering*) and human devastation (*laying waste*) to re-emphasise the irony of the situation: here were women for the first time having a role, however small, in public life and here they were encouraging the most devastating destruction of lives and cities as a result.

The last line has a number of possible interpretations, all compatible with the messages of the early part of the poem. If *Man's skills* were discovered in women, then we also find the same capacity for evil acts (*his vengeance too*). This same phrase could, however, describe the vengeance of men on women; that they only gave them apparent freedom in the hazardous circumstances of making weapons from poisonous materials, and only for the duration of the war. Whichever type of *vengeance* you decide is prominent, Rumens suggests at the end of the poem that there was a design or political intention behind the whole process in the phrase *expediently unlaced*. The word *unlaced* carries a number of different connotations which complement each other. It may be seen as representing the freeing of women from earlier, Victorian, restrictions such as the corsetry (usually laced-up) that restricted their movement. It may also be seen as evoking the poison theme again, suggesting that the lead that the munitions workers were breathing was 'lacing' the air in the way that a murderer might 'lace' someone's drink.

Notes

Where full bibliographical details of a book are not included in the notes they will be found in the bibliography.

Chapter 1

1. Although he is thorough in discussing mainstream poets, Perkins commits the common mistake of virtually ignoring the poetry written by women in this period. This imbalance is addressed in chapters 1 and 2 of Jan Montefiore's book, *Feminism and Poetry* (1987), and it is partly redressed by collections such as *The Faber Book of Twentieth Century Women's Poetry*, ed. Fleur Adcock (1987) and *Bread and Roses*, ed. Diana Scott (1982).

2. From Wordsworth, 'Preface' to *Lyrical Ballads* (1802).

Chapter 2

1. For a thorough and very readable description of the rise of Standard English in its social and historical context, see Leith (1983).

2. For more examples of poetry written in English by black writers, see Paul Breman (ed.) (1973).

3. Prior to the emergence of Standard English and standardised spelling, poetry was automatically written to reflect local pronunciations. There have also been notable dialect writers, such as Robert Burns, in previous centuries. The realism of nineteenth-century novels later encouraged the use of dialect for the speech of certain characters (e.g. Stephen Blackpool in *Hard Times* and Joseph in *Wuthering Heights*). Finally, the twentieth century has seen the conscious use of dialect for a wide range of reasons, many being the 'search for an identity' of oppressed or displaced peoples.

4. See chapter 4 for definitions of the different kinds of word-formation in English.

Chapter 3

1. For a detailed description of the influence of folk culture and

the Irish language on the poetry of Ireland, see Loreto Todd's volume
in this series: *The Language of Irish Literature* (1989).

Chapter 4

1. Wordsworth, 'Preface' to *Lyrical Ballads* (1802).
2. Anthropomorphism is similar to personification, but in this
case, animals are given the characteristics of human beings, often by
the breaking of selectional restrictions on words.
3. Although related to the traditional figure called 'synecdoche',
there is a difference. Here the part is being shown to have similarities
with the whole; in synecdoche, the part is seen to stand symbolically
for the whole.
4. The types of contradictions being used to illustrate this section
are based on collocation alone. Other examples also involve conventional opposites and these are discussed in the last section of
chapter 5.

Chapter 5

1. Notice that *now* and *always*, although often seen as opposites,
each have a more appropriate opposite; *then* and *never* respectively.
This supports that view explained here, that this poem is deliberately
based on a shaky foundation which is dismantled in the final line.

Chapter 7

1. Note that the discussion of second person addressees in poetry
first appeared in 1991 in *Lampshade*, an anthology produced by the
Writing Society at Huddersfield Polytechnic (now the University of
Huddersfield).

Glossary

The glossary aims to make the small amount of technical language used in this book accessible to all readers, irrespective of their previous knowledge. It is therefore very simple in its explanations and may at times 'gloss over' the complications that would be addressed by more specialist books. It is a reading aid rather than a definitive dictionary of linguistic terms. The examples here are all taken from everyday language rather than poetry. First, it was easier to find simple examples which were not from poetry. Secondly, the connection between the creativity of poetry and the creativity of ordinary usage is emphasised by these examples when used alongside the poetic examples in the book.

There is an inevitable circularity in using language to define language. This effect is diminished here by a system of cross-references making explicit the connections between different entries in the glossary. The cross-references are to be found in the final line of the entry, introduced by the arrow symbol →.

adjective
Words such as *bad*, *blue*, *happy* which either premodify nouns as in *the happy music* or occur as complements after verbs like *be* as in *The music was cheerful*. They are sometimes formed from nouns by the addition of a suffix: *careful*, *flashy*, *warlike*.
→ premodifier, complement, suffix

adverb
Words such as *joyfully*, *later*, *home* which usually function as a clause element describing the manner, time or place of the event described by the sentence: ***Later** they all ran **joyfully home***. Many adverbs are formed by adding the *-ly* suffix to adjectives as in *candidly*, *wonderfully*.
→ clause, adjective, suffix

adverbial
The name of the clause element formed by adverbs, but also sometimes formed by prepositional phrases: ***In the morning** we walked **to the boathouse***.
→ clause, adverb

151

affix
Derived words often have a morpheme added to show that they have changed. These may be prefixes, such as **unkind**, **disruptive**, or suffixes, such as *helpful*, *sweeper*. Prefixes and suffixes are jointly known as affixes.
→ morpheme, prefix, suffix

agentive
Nouns derived from verbs, often by the addition of a suffix *-er*, may denote the person (or animal) performing the action of the verb. Thus a *baker* is someone who bakes and a *trier* is someone who tries hard. They are agents of the action.
→ suffix

alliteration
When two or more words close together in a text begin with the same consonant: **muck and magic, bring and buy.** A similar effect is gained even when the consonants are not all at the beginning of words: *limpid pool of liquid.* It is important to remember that alliteration is primarily a sound effect; written consonants which share a sound may therefore be used alliteratively: *surreptitious celebrations.* An extension of alliteration is the use of consonantal sounds which share their manner of articulation as in **nauseating miasma** where there is a mixture of nasal sounds: bilabial /m/, alveolar /n/ and velar/ŋ/.
→ nasal, bilabial, alveolar, velar

alveolar
One of the 'places of articulation' of sounds, involving a closure between the tongue and the alveolar ridge (just behind the front teeth). Examples of alveolar sounds in English are: /t/, /d/, /n/.

anaphoric reference
When there is a connection between two sentences in a text (cohesion), there will usually be a full version in one sentence and a referring item in the next sentence: **The man next-door** *hates cats.* **He** *threw a stone at one yesterday.* As in this example, the normal order is for the full version (*The man next-door*) to occur before the referring item (*He*) and this is known as anaphoric reference.

antonyms
Although we often use this word to mean 'opposites' in everyday English, linguists use it to refer to a particular kind of opposition, known as 'gradable antonymy'.
→ opposites, complementaries, converses

assonance
The concentrated use of the same vowel in a short stretch of text is known as assonance: *try the fine wines from my vine.* The difference between sound and spelling is even more pronounced in the English vowel system than in English consonants, so assonantal vowels may look different more often than alliterative consonants. As with

alliteration, groups of vowel sounds may have a partially assonantal effect. The groupings of vowels which work in this way are high, mid and low vowels on the one hand and front and back vowels on the other.
→ alliteration

auxiliary verb
The subtler modulations of meaning carried by verb endings (inflections) in some European languages are carried instead in English by the auxiliary verbs. These occur before the main verb, and indicate whether, for example, the action is continuous: *he is playing* or whether it is possible, but unlikely: *Sheila might come tomorrow.*
→ inflection, continuous, participle

bilabial
One of the 'places of articulation' of sounds, it is produced by the closure, and subsequent separation of the lips. Examples of bilabial sounds in English are /b/, /p/ and /m/.

cataphoric reference
See first the entry for anaphoric reference. Cataphoric reference is more unusual than anaphoric reference. It occurs where the fuller explanation *follows* the referring item, so that there is some suspense in the text while the reader/hearer waits to discover the identity of the referring item: *They were everywhere. Dogs of all shapes and sizes.* Here it is not until the second sentence that we discover what *they* refers to.
→ anaphoric reference

clause
Although clauses are often sentences in themselves, sometimes sentences consist of more than one clause. A clause will always contain a verb phrase and usually other clause elements such as subjects, objects or adverbials. *When I went home, the dog came to meet me.* Here the adverbial element of the sentence, telling us when the action took place, is a clause rather than a prepositional phrase (such as *in the evening*) or an adverb (such as *afterwards*).
→ verb phrase, subject, object, adverbial, adverb

cohesion
Since texts (whether written or spoken) are clearly not random series of sentences, there must be ways in which the sentences of a text join together to make sense. Cohesion is the term given to this process which is fulfilled in a number of different ways. For example, pronouns are used to refer to people already mentioned in the text, similar words and phrases are used to paraphrase one another and adverbs are used to make relations of place, time or causation explicit. See the beginning of chapter 7 for a fuller explanation.
→ adverb

collocation, collocates
Words which only occur with a very limited range of other words are described as having a restricted collocational range: *stark naked* but not *stark nude*; *dinner service* and *tea service* but not *breakfast service*. There are frequently occurring words, such as the verb *be* and the conjunction *and* which can collocate with almost any other word, but most words fall between these two extremes. The interest of collocational range for creative uses of English is that words with restricted collocations can evoke their collocates even when they do not occur in the text. Thus *stark* brings *naked* and *staring mad* to mind, even when used without these words.
→ selectional restrictions

comparative adjective
When adjectives have a meaning which is gradable, they may have two inflected forms, comparative and superlative, created by the addition of the inflectional suffixes *-er* and *-est*: *mean, meaner, meanest*.
→ adjective, inflection, suffix, superlative adjective

complement
A clause element which occurs after verbs like *be* and gives some information about the subject or object of the sentence. The complement may be a noun phrase as in *Susan is **a teacher*** or adjectival as in *She is **very clever***. Examples showing object complements are: *The war made John **a wiser man*** and *My experience made me **sad***.
→ clause, subject, object, noun phrase

complementaries
This kind of opposition concerns words which are mutually exclusive in their meaning. You cannot, for example, be both *dead* and *alive* at the same time, or both *male* and *female*. Although we may use expressions that make these opposites seem to be gradable, such as *I feel half-dead*, they are treated most of the time as non-gradable meanings.
→ opposites, converses, gradable antonyms

compounding
Compound words are created from two or more independent words (free morphemes). They will usually belong to the word-class of the last word in the sequence. In *blackbird*, for example, the resulting compound is in the class of nouns alongside *bird* itself. It is sometimes difficult to distinguish between compounds and phrases, but poets often hyphenate those inventions that they perceive as compounds.
→ morpheme

conjunction
The main conjunctions in English are *and*, *but* and *or*. They join together units of all sizes and levels, from nouns as in *fish **and** chips* and noun phrases as in *the woman in white **and** the man in blue* to clauses as in *I want a cup of tea **but** she wants a half of lager*.
→ noun phrase

connotation
There is usually a consensus within society about the meaning of a word and this consensus corresponds to the word's denotation. Most words also have attached to them a number of connotations, some of which are individual and some of which are more widely recognised. Some of the connotations which are shared by speakers attach a level of formality to a word. *Powder Room* and *loo*, for example, are at opposite ends of the formality scale. Other kinds of connotation give the word a flavour of the place it comes from as is seen from the Scots word *haggis*. Or a word may be associated with a particular group of people; many words, such as *choo-choo* or *teddy* are associated with young children and their parents.

continuous participle
See *-ing* forms.

converses
These opposites view the relationship they share from different angles. *Buying*, for example, is one way of viewing a commercial transaction whereas *selling* approaches the transaction from the seller's point of view. These opposites depend on one another; there can be no *husband* without a *wife*, no *giving* without *receiving*.
→ opposites, complementaries, gradable antonyms

derivation
Derived words are usually formed by the addition of an affix to the stem word. Apart from derivations formed with prefixes (e.g. *unhelpful*), derived words change their word-class. So verbs can become nouns as in *deprive* – *deprivation* and nouns can become verbs as in *nationalise*. Other word-classes can also be changed.
→ affix, prefix, suffix

determiner
The class of words that occurs at the beginning of noun phrases, before any premodifying adjectives and the head noun: *the last time*. The most common determiners are the articles, *the* and *a(n)*, but others include *this*, *these*, *that*, *those*, *all*, *several*.
→ noun phrase, premodifier, adjective

dialect
A variety of a language which is associated with a particular geographical or social speech community. They may be widespread (Standard English is a dialect spoken all over the world) or they may be spoken by very few people as in a small rural village. Dialects have their own vocabulary and grammar and are sometimes also associated with a particular accent.

diphthongs
Many of the vowel sounds in English words are diphthongs. They involve a change in the shape of the mouth during the pronunciation of the vowel, making the sound modulate accordingly. One example

of an English diphthong is /ai/, found in the words *bright* and *wine*. This diphthong moves from an open back vowel, /a/, to a closed front vowel, /i/.

-ed form
This term is sometimes used to refer to the regular past tense form of verbs in English. Examples include *banged* and *brushed*.

embedded clauses
→ subordinate clauses

-en form
Although most past participles in English have the same form as the past tense (ending in *-ed*) the verbs which distinguish the participle from the past tense use the suffix *-en*: *broken, spoken*. To distinguish grammatically between past tense and participle, the term *-en* is used for all participle forms, even when the form is actually *-ed*: *I have crashed the car (-en)*. All participles occur either following an auxiliary verb as in *it was broken* and *he will be asked* or they are used as though they were adjectives: *the broken vase*.
→ auxiliary verb

end-focus
The important information in an English sentence usually occurs toward the end of the clause, on the last obligatory clause element: *He ate a banana*. This is known as *end-focus*.
→ clause, obligatory element

finite verb
Verbs which carry tense and agree with the subject are finite verbs: *I walk* and *she sings* but not *walking* or *sung*.
→ subject

focus
→ end-focus

free verse
Poetry not structured according to strict metrical and rhyming patterns.

fricative
One of the manners of articulation of consonants. Fricatives are produced from the sound of the air passing through a constriction somewhere in the vocal tract. Examples of English fricatives are /f/, /v/, /s/, /z/.

fronting, fronted
Sometimes the usual order of clause elements is changed by moving one of the elements to the beginning of the sentence: *Hungry I wasn't!* Here the fronting of the adjective *hungry* shifts the end-focus to the negative verb rather than remaining on the complement.
→ clause, adjective, end-focus, complement

gradable antonyms
The most common type of opposite in English. Gradable antonyms have many shades of meaning between their extremes and in some cases there are intermediate pairs of antonyms: *hot* and *cold*, *warm* and *cool*.
→ opposites, complementaries, converses

homograph
Homographs are words which are spelt the same but sound different: *lead* (to take the dog for a walk) and *lead* (roofing material).

homonym
Homonyms are words which both look the same written down and sound the same when spoken: *alight* (get off a vehicle) and *alight* (to be burning).

homophone
Homophones are words which sound the same but are spelt differently: *faint* (swoon) and *feint* (lines ruled on paper).

iambic pattern
Traditionally English poetry was written in a metrical pattern which alternated unstressed and stressed syllables. The most common number of iambic 'feet' (unstressed syllable followed by stressed) in a line of verse was five: *I wánt to wásh my háir and gó to béd.*

indefinite article
The indefinite article is *a* (or *an*). It is one of the class of determiners.
→ determiners

infinitive
The form of the verb which is entered in a dictionary and sometimes occurs with *to: (to) be, (to) sing, (to) laugh.*

inflection
The major word-classes, nouns, adjectives, verbs and adverbs all have a small number of inflections which may be suffixed to their stem form. The plural morpheme, for example, may be added to nouns: *cats, dogs, horses.* The past tense morpheme is added to most verbs: *touched, surprised.* There are exceptions in all of the classes: *one sheep / two sheep* (no suffix for plural), *I cut (today) / I cut (yesterday).*
→ noun adjective, verb, morpheme

-ing participle
English verbs show continuity of action by the use of the auxiliary verb *be* followed by the main verb with an *-ing* inflection: *I am writing, she was crying.* Sometimes called the continuous participle.
→ verb phrase, auxiliary verb, inflection

internal rhyme
Internal rhyme occurs when rhyming words are placed not at the ends of lines of verse, but on the same line: *I stared at the green screen.*

inversion
When the order of two clause elements is reversed: *glad that I live am I*. Here the subject of the verb, *I*, has changed places with the complement, *glad that I live*.
→ clause, subject, complement

lexical field
Groups of words which share some aspects of their meaning. This term can be used loosely to refer to vocabulary sets, such as words associated with food: *butter, cheese, eggs*, etc. It is more frequently used for groups which are partial synonyms and share a large proportion of their meaning: *beg, beseech, plead*.
→ partial synonyms

liquid
One of the manners of articulation, sometimes also called semi-vowels. These sounds involve an incomplete closure in the vocal tract and are therefore less sharp in their sound than other consonants, but more distinct than vowels which are produced by the general shape of the oral cavity. Examples of English liquids are: /r/, /l/, /w/, /j/.

morphemes
A morpheme is the smallest unit that has meaning. It may be the same length as a word, as in *car* or *dance*. On the other hand, many of the inflectional and derivational suffixes in English are also morphemes. The plural morpheme is an inflection: *train*s, so is the comparative morpheme: *brav*er.
→ inflection, derivation, suffix

morphology
The structure of English words according to their morphemes, and the study of such structure, is known as morphology.

nasal
One of the manners of articulation of consonants. These sounds are produced by the simultaneous release of air through the mouth and through the nose. Examples of English nasal sounds are: /m/, /n/, /ŋ/.

noun phrase
Functioning in the same way as nouns themselves, noun phrases may have a number of premodifiers before the head noun, including determiners, participles and adjectives: ***the green swinging** gate*. The head noun (*gate*) may also be followed by prepositional phrases and/or subordinate clauses: *the gate **in the meadow that I was sitting on***.
→ premodifier, participle, adjective, subordinate clause

noun phrase in apposition
Sometimes two nouns, or noun phrases, are used to refer equally to the same referent: *Mr Bones, the butcher*.
→ noun phrase

object
Objects usually follow the verb phrase and are often affected in some way by the action of the verb. They are most commonly noun phrases, but may also be subordinate clauses: *I washed **the cup**, Jenny decided **where to go**.*
→ verb phrase, clause, noun phrase, subordinate clause

obligatory element
Each clause element is either obligatory or optional in a clause. Omission of obligatory elements undermines the grammaticality of the clause. The choice of verb usually determines which elements are obligatory. Thus a verb of movement will often require an adverbial of place in the clause: *Fred ran **to the shops***, while such adverbials are usually optional with, for example, verbs of talking: *Joe told him a story **in the garden***.
→ clause, optional element, adverbial

onomatopeia
Words which echo the sound the word refers to are onomatopoeic. They are often words which appeal to children, such as *moo, neigh, baa*. More mature onomatopoeic words in English include *clap, jingle, thud*.

opposites
While we are all aware that some words have opposites (*good – bad, happy – sad*), there are different types of opposites.
→ gradable antonyms, complementaries, converses

optional element
See obligatory element. Most optional elements are adverbials which add information about time, place, cause, etc. without being essential to the structure.
→ obligatory element, adverbial

palatal
One of the places of articulation of consonants. Palatal sounds are produced by the central section of the tongue touching the hard palate. English palatal sounds are: /ʃ/, /ʒ/, /tʃ/ and /dʒ/.

partial synonyms
Members of lexical fields are often close enough in meaning to be called partial synonyms. Examples of movement verbs which are partially synonymous are: *sprint, trot, jog*.
→ lexical field

participial adjective, noun
Verbs have two participle forms: *-ing* and *-en* forms. Most participle forms may be used in the same way as adjectives, premodifying a noun as in *the weeping willow* or after the verb *be* as in *the glass was broken anyway*. Participles, like *weeping*, which are commonly used in this way often acquire a more restricted meaning, resulting

from their range of collocates, than their verbal counterpart.
→ participle, premodifier, collocation

participle
→ *-en form* and *-ing form.*

phonological
The study of human speech sounds is known as 'phonetics'. The study
of the sound system of a particular language is called phonology.

polysemy, polysemous
When a lexical item has two or more meanings which are related to
each other, but different enough to warrant a separate mention in the
dictionary, it is polysemous.

postposed
See also entries for inversion and fronted. The positioning of clause
elements toward the end of the structure, when they would normally
occur earlier. The sentence *In walked Mr Murray*, for example, post-
poses the subject, *Mr Murray*, and fronts the adverbial, *in*. The effect
is to place the end-focus on the subject rather than on the adverbial.
→ clause, subject, adverbial

prefix
An affix occurring before the stem of the word: ***ungracious***, ***disgrace-
ful***, ***reiterate***.
→ affix, suffix

premodifier
Any determiner, number, adjective, participle or noun which occurs
in a noun phrase before the head noun: ***the six vigorous climbing
rose*** bushes.
→ noun phrase, adjective, participle

pronominal reference
One of the cohesive features of texts, pronominal reference involves
the use of pronouns to refer to people and things already introduced
in the text: *Ms Adams went for a walk.* ***She*** *took the dog with* ***her***.
→ cohesion

prosodic
The 'tunes' we use, superimposed on the words spoken, are part of
the prosodic system of the language. Also called intonation.

referent
When a word refers to something in the 'real world', the term 'referent' is used to identify the non-linguistic part of this connection.
Many words, of course, have no obvious referent or have only comparative reference: *tall* (how tall?), *my* (whose?).

reverse rhyme
Syllables beginning with the same consonant cluster and followed by
the same vowel: *shorn/short, plain/plate, fish/fingers*.

selectional restrictions
Similar to restricted collocation, but less arbitrary. Some words have general semantic restrictions on the words that can occur with them. For example, adjectives and verbs of emotion are usually restricted to occur with human (or at least animate) subjects: *the divorce **upset** her, the little boy was **sad**.*
→ collocation, adjective, subject

semantics
The study of meanings; for this book mainly restricted to word meaning.

semantic features
Word meanings are sometimes analysed into 'features' in order to compare more effectively the meanings of different words.

semi-vowel
→ liquids

sense
One of the polysemous meanings of a word.
→ polysemy

sibilant
One of the manners of articulation of consonants. A sub-group of the fricatives, sibilants involve friction of air passing through a small opening caused by a groove in the tongue. The English sibilants are: /s/, /z/, /ʃ/, /ʒ/.
→ fricative

sound symbolism
When a small group of words share some part of their meaning and also part of their sound/spelling, the sounds take on the features of shared meaning. For example, the words *sneer, snide, sneaky* share the *sn-* consonant cluster, which therefore seems to symbolise the 'nasty' aspect of their meaning.

standard language, Standard English
Many languages have a standard, or various standard forms, which are used for official functions, the written language, the mass media, etc. Standard languages usually exist alongside other dialects of the language and/or other local languages.

subject
The clause element which usually occurs before the verb and with which the verb phrase agrees in person and number. Most commonly a noun or noun phrase: ***coffee** is good for you, **chocolates** are bad for you.*
→ clause, noun phrase

subordinate clause
Clauses which function as only part of the sentence and are not

main clauses which can stand alone. Relative clauses, for example, occur within noun phrases, after the head noun: *the house **where I was born**. . . .*

suffix
An affix which is placed after the stem of the word.
→ affix, prefix

superlative adjective
The inflection of adjectives which expresses the most extreme form of the quality indicated by the adjective concerned: *the **greatest** test yet, the **longest** river in the world.*
→ adjective

syllabic metre
Some poetry is structured on the basis of stanzas in which corresponding lines haves the same number of syllables. For example, the first line in each stanza may have seven syllables, the second ten syllables, and so on.

transitive
Verbs which require a following object are transitive: *I **broke the plate**.*
→ object

uncountable
Nouns are divided into two categories: countable and uncountable (or mass and count). Uncountable nouns refer, for example, to *sugar, air, water*; masses that cannot easily be divided into countable units.

velar
One of the places of articulation of consonants involving contact between the back of the tongue and the soft palate or 'velum'. Velar sounds in English are: /g/, /k/, /ŋ/.

verb phrase
Verbs in English may have their meaning modulated by up to four auxiliary verbs: *I **might have been being** beaten.* The resulting combination of auxiliary verbs and main verb is called the verb phrase.
→ auxiliary verb

voiced
Many pairs of consonantal sound are differentiated only by their voicing or voicelessness. Voicing occurs when the vocal cords are partially closed as the air emerges from the lungs and vibrations results. In English all vowels are voiced, as are all liquid and nasal consonants and the following plosives and fricatives: /b/, /d/, /g/, /v/, /ð/, /z/, /ʒ/.

voiceless
→ voiced

zero-derivation
Some words in the major classes (nouns, verbs, adjectives, adverbs) change word-class without the normal process of affixation: *plaster* (n.) – *plaster* (v.).
→ adjective, adverb, affix

References: Poetry

The following list contains references to all the twentieth-century poems (and in some cases poetry books) mentioned or quoted in this volume. The entries are listed alphabetically by poet, but where there is a list of poems by one writer, these are listed in order of appearance in the text. The brackets at the end of each entry refer to the Poetry section of the main Bibliography and give readers the opportunity to look up the whole poem from which quotations are taken. Where the brackets contain multiple references, the poem(s) concerned can be found in all of the volumes cited.

ADAMS, ANNA, *Unrecorded Speech* (Scott,1982).
ADCOCK, FLEUR, *Against Coupling* (Morrison and Motion, 1982).
ANYIDOHO, KOFI, *My Mailman Friend was Here* (Anyidoho, 1984).
ARMITAGE, JENNIFER, *To Our Daughter* (Scott, 1982).
ATWOOD, MARGARET, *Woman Skating* (Adcock, 1987).
AUDEN, W. H.,
   The Geography of the House (Macbeth, 1979);
   On the Circuit (Macbeth, 1979);
   Moon Landing, (Mendelson, 1979);
   Streams (Wollman, 1957);
   O Love . . . (Wollman, 1957);
   1st September 1939 (Wollman, 1957; Skelton, 1964);
   To a Writer on His Birthday (Skelton, 1964);
   Spain (Skelton, 1964);
   Consider (Macbeth, 1979);
   The Dream (Skelton, 1964);
   Musée des Beaux Arts (Wollman, 1957; Macbeth, 1979);
   Lay your sleeping head my love . . . (Wollman, 1957; Skelton, 1964).
BELLERBY, FRANCES, *Bereaved Child's First Night* (Adcock, 1987).
BENNETT, LOUISE, *Colonization in Reverse* (Burnett, 1986).
BERRYMAN, JOHN, *New Year's Eve* (Alvarez, 1962).
BETJEMAN, JOHN,
   The Executive (Macbeth, 1979);
   A Subaltern's Love Song (Macbeth, 1979);
   In Westminster Abbey (Skelton, 1964);
   Upper Lambourne (Heath-Stubbs, 1953).
bissett, bill, *th wundrfulness uv th mountees our secret police* (Bowering,1984).

BLACKBURN, THOMAS, *Hospital for Defectives* (Allott, 1982).
BROOKS, GWENDOLYN, *The Mother* (Adcock, 1987).
CAMERON, NORMAN, *Public-House Confidence* (Skelton, 1964).
CHARLES, FAUSTIN, *Sugar Cane* (Burnett, 1986).
CLAMPITT, AMY, *A Hairline Fracture* (Clampitt, 1984).
CLIFTON, LUCILLE, *The Lost Baby Poem* (Raving Beauties, 1983).
COGHILL, MARY, *Knowing* (Scott, 1982).
COOPER, JANE, *El Sueño de la Razón (Adcock, 1987).*
COPE, WENDY, Depression (Adcock, 1987).
CORNFORD, FRANCES, *To a Fat Lady Seen from the Train* (Adcock, 1987).
CRICHTON SMITH, IAN, *Old Woman* (Lucie-Smith, 1970).
cummings, e. e.,
    'love is more thicker than forget' (cummings, 1960);
    'in Just/ spring' (cummings, 1960);
    'death having lost put on his universe' (cummings, 1960);
    'anyone lived in a pretty how town' (cummings, 1960);
    'all ignorance toboggans into know' (cummings, 1960).
CUNNAE, PATRICK, *If Russians didn't exist we'd have to invent them* (Hoy, 1986).
DABYDEEN, DAVID, *Slave Song* (Burnett, 1986).
DOBSON, ROSEMARY, *The Fever*, Country Press (Adcock, 1987).
DORCEY, MARY, *First Love* (Scott, 1982).
DUNN, DOUGLAS,
    Sunday Morning Among the Houses of Terry Street (Dunn, 1986);
    Modern Love (Dunn, 1986; Morrison and Motion, 1982);
    A Removal from Terry Street (Dunn, 1986; Morrison and Motion, 1982);
    The Kaleidoscope (Dunn, 1986).
DURRELL, LAWRENCE, *Deus Loci* (Allott, 1982).
ELIOT, T.S.
    The Waste Land (Eliot, 1963);
    Ash-Wednesday (Allott, 1982);
    Little Gidding (Macbeth, 1979);
    Rhapsody on a Windy Night (Macbeth, 1979);
    Whispers of Immortality (Macbeth, 1979);
    The Hollow Men (Macbeth, 1979);
    The Love Song of Alfred J. Prufrock (Macbeth, 1979).
FEINSTEIN, ELAINE, *Calliope in the labour ward* (Scott, 1982)v
FINCH, VIVIEN, *Green Ice (Scott, 1982).*
FRASER, KONNY, Nuclear defence query (Hoy, 1986).
FROST, ROBERT, *Mending Wall* (Wollman, 1957).
GALLAGHER, TESS, *Black Silk* (Adcock, 1987).
GINSBERG, ALLEN, *Howl* (Ginsberg, 1984).
GLÜCK, LOUISE, *For my sister, The Gift* (Adcock, 1987).
GRAVES, ROBERT, *Warning to Children* (Allott, 1982).
GRIGSON, GEOFFREY, *And Forgetful of Europe* (Skelton, 1964).
GUNN, THOM, *On the Move* (Macbeth, 1979; Allott, 1982).

GUTTERIDGE, BERNARD, *Home Revisited* (Skelton, 1964).
HARRIS, CLAIRE, *The Conception of Winter* (Harris, 1989).
HARRISON, TONY,
  Next Door (Harrison, 1984);
  Long Distance (Morrison and Motion, 1982);
  Illuminations (Harrison, 1984);
  Book Ends – I (Morrison and Motion, 1982);
  Them & [uz] (Harrison, 1984);
  Timer (Morrison and Motion, 1982).
HEANEY, SEAMUS, *Funeral Rites, The Harvest Bow* (Morrison and Motion, 1982).
HEATH-STUBBS, JOHN, *A Charm against the Toothache* (Allott, 1982; Lucie-Smith, 1970).
HENRI, ADRIAN, *Batpoem, Without You, Don't Worry Everything's Going to be All Right, The New, Fast, Automatic Daffodils* (Henri, 1986).
HEWITT, PETER, *Place of Birth* (Skelton, 1964).
HILL, GEOFFREY, *Canticle for Good Friday* (Alvarez, 1962).
HOLLOWAY, JOHN, *Warning to a Guest* (Allott, 1982).
HOROWITZ, FRANCES, *The Messenger* (Scott, 1982).
HORTON, GEORGE MOSES, *The Poet's Feeble Petition* (Breman, 1973).
HUGHES, TED, *Thrushes, Hawk Roosting, Wind, View of a Pig* (Alvarez, 1962).
HUXLEY, ALDOUS, *Second Philosopher's Song* (Allott, 1982).
JACKOWSKA, NICKI, *Family Outing – A Celebration* (Scott, 1982).
JOHNSON, LINTON KWESI, *Reggae fi Dada* (Burnett, 1986).
JONG, ERICA, *Woman Enough* (Raving Beauties, 1983).
JOSEPH, JENNY, *The Lost Continent* (Scott, 1982).
KUMIN, MAXINE, *The Excrement Poem* (Adcock, 1987).
LANCASTER, JOHN, *The Locker* (Lancaster, 1986).
LARKIN, JOAN, *'Vagina' Sonnet* (Raving Beauties, 1983).
LARKIN, PHILIP,
  Mr Bleaney (Lucie-Smith, 1970; Larkin, 1964);
  Essential Beauty (Larkin, 1964);
  Church Going (Macbeth, 1979);
  XXVII (Larkin, 1966);
  VI (Larkin, 1966);
  Broadcast (Larkin, 1964);
  As Bad as a Mile (Larkin, 1964);
  Talking in Bed (Larkin, 1964);
  Afternoons (Larkin, 1964);
  Ambulances (Macbeth, 1979; Larkin, 1964);
  The Importance of Elsewhere (Larkin, 1964);
  Love Songs in Age (Larkin, 1964);
  Nothing to be Said (Larkin, 1964);
  Naturally the Foundation (Larkin, 1964);
  Water (Macbeth, 1979; Larkin, 1964);
  XXX (Larkin, 1966);

Lines on a Young Lady's Photograph Album (Allott, 1982).

LAWRENCE, D. H.,
  Snake (Macbeth, 1979);
  The Humming Bird (Macbeth, 1979);
  Bavarian Gentians (Macbeth, 1979);
  The Mosquito (Allott, 1982).

LEE, LAURIE, *Music in a Spanish Town* (Skelton, 1964).

LESTER, JULIUS, *On the birth of my son, Malcolm Coltrane* (Breman, 1973).

LEWIS, C. DAY, *You that Love England* (Allott, 1982).

LONGLEY, MICHAEL, *Swans Mating* (Morrison and Motion, 1982).

LOWELL, ROBERT, *Life Studies* (Lowell, 1959).

MaCNEICE, LOUIS,
  Autumn Journal (part VI) (Skelton, 1964);
  Birmingham (Skelton, 1964);
  Snow (Macbeth, 1979; Allott, 1982);
  Poem (Skelton, 1964);
  Autumn Journal (part III) (Skelton, 1964);
  London Rain (Skelton, 1964);
  The Lake in the Park (Auden, 1964).

MALCOM, BARBARA, *Bedtime Story* (Breman, 1973).

MCGOUGH, ROGER,
  First Day at School (McGough, 1976);
  War of the Roses (McGough, 1979);
  The Commission (McGough, 1976);
  Let Me Die a Youngman's Death (Lucie-Smith, 1970);
  ofa sunday (McGough, 1973);
  The Lesson (McGough, 1976).

MCGUCKIAN, MEBDH, *The Weaver Girl* (Morrison and Motion, 1982).

MEW, CHARLOTTE, *In Nunhead Cemetery* (Adcock, 1987).

MILES, JOSEPHINE, *Summer* (Adcock, 1987).

MILLAY, EDNA ST VINCENT, *Childhood is the Kingdom Where Nobody Dies, Passer Mortuus Est, Sonnet xxiv* (Adcock, 1987).

MITCHELL, ELMA, *Thoughts after Ruskin* (Adcock, 1987).

MORRIS, MERVYN, *To an Expatriate Friend* (Burnett, 1986).

MOTION, ANDREW, *Bathing at Glymenopoulo* (Morrison and Motion, 1982).

MUIR, EDWIN, *The Combat, The Confirmation* (Wollman, 1957).

MUTABARUKA, *Free Up de Lan, White Man* (Burnett, 1986).

NICHOL, bp, *Against Explanation* (Bowering, 1984).

NORMAN, ROSEMARY, *My son and I* (Scott, 1982).

OWEN, WILFRED,
  Dulce et Decorum Est (Heath-Stubbs, 1953; Macbeth, 1979);
  Strange Meeting (Allott, 1982; Macbeth, 1979);
  Exposure (Allott, 1982).

PIERCY, MARGE,
  Rape Poem (Raving Beauties, 1983);
  The Woman in the Ordinary (Raving Beauties, 1983);

In the Men's Room(s) (Raving Beauties, 1983);
Mornings in various years (Piercy, 1983).

PLATH, SYLVIA,
Morning Song (Raving Beauties, 1983);
Poppies in July (Adcock, 1987);
You're (Adcock, 1987);
Mushrooms (Adcock, 1987).

RAINE, CRAIG, *The Grocer* (Morrison and Motion, 1982).

REDGROVE, PETER, *Old House* (Alvarez, 1962).

REID, CHRISTOPHER, *Parable of Geometric Progression* (Morrison and Motion, 1982).

RICH, ADRIENNE,
Transcendental Etude (Rich, 1978);
Waking in the Dark (Adcock, 1987);
Snapshots of a Daughter-in-Law (Adcock, 1987).

RIDLER, ANNE, *At Parting* (Allott, 1982).

ROBERTS, MICHAEL, *The Secret Springs, The Child* (Skelton, 1964).

RUMENS, CAROL, *A Poem for Chessmen, The Freedom Won by War for Women* (Morrison and Motion, 1982).

SASSOON, SIEGFRIED, *The Death Bed, The Child at the Window* (Allott, 1982).

SCARFE, FRANCIS, *Progression* (Skelton, 1964).

SCOTT, DENNIS, *Weaponsong* (Burnett, 1986).

SHORT, JOHN, *Carol* (Skelton, 1964; Heath-Stubbs, 1953).

SHUTTLE, PENELOPE, *Downpour* (Morrison and Motion, 1982).

SIMPSON, LOUIS, *Back in the States* (Burnett, 1986).

SMITH, STEVIE, *I rode with my darling* (Scott, 1982).

SPENDER, STEPHEN,
Port Bou (Skelton, 1964);
Ultima Ratio Regum (Skelton, 1964);
Fall of a City (Skelton, 1964);
An Elementary School Classroom in a Slum (Skelton, 1964);
Rough (Spender, 1965);
The Pylons (Skelton, 1964);
The Double Shame (Allott, 1982).

STEVENSON, ANNE,
Correspondences (Morrison and Motion, 1982);
Giving Rabbit to my Cat Bonnie (Adcock, 1987);
By the Boat House, Oxford (Adcock, 1987).

ST JOHN, BRUCE, *Bajan Litany* (Burnett, 1986).

THOMAS, DYLAN,
Fern Hill (Macbeth, 1979);
Poem in October (Macbeth, 1979; Allott, 1982);
And Death Shall Have No Dominion (Skelton, 1964; Macbeth, 1979).

THOMAS, EDWARD, *The Owl* (Heath-Stubbs, 1953).

THOMAS, R. S.,
Poetry For Supper (Macbeth, 1979);

Welsh Landscape (Alvarez, 1962);
Evans (Alvarez, 1962; Macbeth, 1979);
Tramp (Macbeth, 1979).

WALEY, ARTHUR, *The Chrysanthemums in the Eastern Garden* (Allott, 1982).

WRIGHT, JUDITH, *Request to a Year* (Adcock, 1987).

YEATS, W. B.,
The Song of Wandering Aengus (Jeffares, 1974);
Fergus and the Druid (Jeffares, 1974);
Cuchulain's Fight with the Sea (Jeffares, 1974);
The Second Coming (Wollman, 1957; Macbeth, 1979; Jeffares, 1974);
Byzantium (Wollman, 1957; Macbeth, 1979; Jeffares, 1974).

Bibliography

Poetry

ADCOCK, F. (ed.), *The Faber Book of Twentieth Century Women's Poetry* (London: Faber and Faber, 1987).

ALLOTT, K. (ed.), *English Poetry 1918–60* (Harmondsworth: Penguin Books, 2nd edn, 1962; present title, 1982).

ALVAREZ, A. (ed.), *The New Poetry* (Harmondsworth: Penguin Books, 1962).

ANYIDOHO, K., *A Harvest of Our Dreams* (London: Heinemann, 1984).

AUDEN, W.H. (ed.), *Selected Poems of Louis MacNeice* (London: Faber and Faber, 1964).

BOWERING, G. (ed.), *The Contemporary Canadian Poem Anthology* (Toronto: The Coach House Press, 1984).

BURNETT, P. (ed.), *The Penguin Book of Caribbean Verse in English* (Harmondsworth: Penguin Books, 1986).

BUSH, D. (ed.), *Milton Poetical Works* (Oxford: OUP, 1966).

BREMAN, P. (ed.), *You Better Believe It* (Harmondsworth: Penguin Books, 1973).

CARR, S., *The Batsford Book of Romantic Poetry* (London: Batsford, 1982).

CLAMPITT, A., *The Kingfisher* (London: Faber and Faber, 1984).

cummings, e.e., *Selected Poems 1923–1958* (London: Faber and Faber, 1960).

DUNN, D., *Selected Poems 1964–1983* (London: Faber and Faber, 1986).

ELLIOT, T.S., *Collected Poems 1909–1962* (London: Faber and Faber, 1963).

GARDNER, H. (ed.), *The Metaphysical Poets* (Harmondsworth: Penguin Books, 1957).

GINSBERG, A., *Howl* (New York: Harper & Row, 1956).

HARRIS, C., *The Conception of Winter* (Williams-Wallace, 1989).

HARRISON, T., *Tony Harrison Selected Poems* (Harmondsworth: Penguin Books, 1984).

HEATH-STUBBS, J. and D. WRIGHT (eds), *The Faber Book of Twentieth Century Verse* (London: Faber and Faber, 1953).

HENRI, A., *Collected Poems 1967–85* (London: Allison & Busby, 1986).

170

HOY, L. (ed.), *Poems for Peace* (London: Pluto Press, 1986).
JEFFARES, N. (ed.) *Yeats Selected Poetry* (London: Macmillan, 1962; Pan Books, 1974).
LANCASTER, J., *Effects of War* (Lancaster: Giant Steps, 1986).
LARKIN, P., *The Whitsun Weddings* (London: Faber and Faber, 1964).
LARKIN, P., *The North Ship* (London: Faber and Faber, 1966).
LOWELL, R., *Life Studies* (London: Faber & Faber, 1959).
LUCIE-SMITH, E. (ed.), *British Poetry since 1945* (Harmondsworth: Penguin Books, 1970, 1985).
MACBETH, G. (ed.), *Poetry 1900 to 1975* (Harlow: Longman, 1979).
MCGOUGH, R., *Gig* (London: Jonathan Cape, 1973).
MCGOUGH, R., *In the Classroom* (London: Jonathan Cape, 1976).
MCGOUGH, R., *Holiday on Death Row* (London: Jonathan Cape, 1979).
MENDELSON, E. (ed.), *W. H. Auden Selected Poems* (London: Faber and Faber, 1979).
MORRISON, B. and A. MOTION (eds), *The Penguin Book of Contemporary British Poetry* (Harmondsworth: Penguin Books, 1982).
PIERCY, M., *Stone, Paper, Knife* (London: Pandora Press, 1983).
POLLARD, A.J., *Silver Poets of the Eighteenth Century* (London: Dent, 1976).
RAVING BEAUTIES (eds), *In the Pink* (London: The Women's Press, 1983).
RICH, A., *The Dream of a Common Language* (New York: Norton, 1978).
SCOTT, D. (ed.), *Bread and Roses* (London: Virago Press, 1982).
SILKIN, J. (ed.), *The Penguin Book of First World War Poetry* (Harmondsworth: Penguin Books, 2nd edn, 1979).
SKELTON, R. (ed.), *Poetry of the Thirties* (Harmondsworth: Penguin Books, 1964).
SPENDER, S., *Selected Poems* (London: Faber and Faber, 1965).
THOMAS, R.S., *R. S. Thomas Selected Poems 1946–1968* (Newcastle upon Tyne: Bloodaxe Books, 1986).
WOLLIMAN, M. (ed.), *Ten Twentieth-century Poets* (London: Harrap, 1957).

Histories, Commentaries and Theoretical Works

BERNIKOW, L. (ed.), *The World Split Open – Women Poets 1552–1950* (London: The Women's Press, 1979).
CHINWEIZU, O. JEMIE and I. MADUBUIKE, *Toward the Decolonization of African Literature* (London: KPI, 1985).
GARRETT, J., *British Poetry Since the Sixteenth Century* (Basingstoke: Macmillan, 1986).
GOODWIN, K., *Understanding African Poetry* (London: Heinemann, 1982).
HOROVITZ, M. (ed.), *Poetry of the 'Underground' in Britain* (Harmondsworth: Penguin Books, 1969).

172   THE LANGUAGE OF TWENTIETH-CENTURY POETRY

LEITH, D., *A Social History of English* (London: Routledge, 1983).
MONTEFIORE, J., *Feminism and Poetry* (London: Pandora Press, 1987).
NWOGA, D.I., *Literature and Modern West African Culture* (Benin: Ethiope Publishing Corporation, 1978).
PERKINS, D., *A History of Modern Poetry*, vol. 1 (Cambridge, Mass.: Belknap Press, 1976).
PERKINS, D., *A History of Modern Poetry*, vol. 2 (Cambridge, Mass.: Belknap Press, 1987).
TODD, L., *The Language of Irish Literature* (Basingstoke: Macmillan, 1989).

Index

173